Homer's Odyssey

Homer's Odyssey

Mitch Grinter & Brendan Dando

CENTURY

1 3 5 7 9 10 8 6 4 2

Century
20 Vauxhall Bridge Road
London SW1V 2SA

Century is part of the Penguin Random House group of companies
whose addresses can be found at global.penguinrandomhouse.com.

Penguin
Random House
UK

First published in 2017 by Century

www.penguin.co.uk

A CIP catalogue record for this book is available from the British Library.

ISBN 9781780898261

Typeset in 12/14.75 pt Sabon by Jouve (UK), Milton Keynes
Printed and bound in Great Britain by Clays Ltd, St Ives Plc

Penguin Random House is committed to a sustainable
future for our business, our readers and our planet. This book is
made from Forest Stewardship Council® certified paper.

MIX
Paper from
responsible sources
FSC
www.fsc.org
FSC® C018179

Dedicated to our parents, who loved us as children, and our wives, who never asked us to grow up.

Foreword

Have you ever heard that quote that goes something like, 'Find a job you love and you will never work a day in your life'? It's true, I am proof of that. Although my job is not without deadlines, some stress at times, and hard work, I wouldn't trade it for anything. I love it. I love what I do and I am so happy and grateful.

My adventure on *The Simpsons* began in 2005, when I was hired as the receptionist at a production company. Nine months into the job, having made some friends who worked on *The Simpsons*, a position for a production assistant in their design department opened up. I jumped at the chance to apply. I was hired and it changed my life. I have since been promoted several times, most recently to production supervisor. I have learned so much along the way, and I still learn things every day. I have met some of my best friends working on this show. I work with some of the most amazing and talented people on the planet. I got to see the animation process change from paper to digital. I am so proud to be part of something that is such a part of TV history. If you would have told 10-year-old me that I would be working on a show I watched and loved so much, I would have said you were crazy. I had no idea I would end up here, but I am so glad that I did. Everything happens for a reason, right? I believe I landed exactly where I was supposed to be.

It means so much to me to be part of *The Simpsons*. Every day (well, Monday through Friday at least) I get to wake up and help make one of the most important and relevant animated series ever. That to me is so magical. It really means the world to me to be so lucky. Everything really *is* coming up Milhouse!

I am so excited for you to have this book in your hands! It's such a love letter to a show that has had an impact on so many lives. Brendan and Mitch are *Simpsons* experts and two devoted fans. The *Four Finger Discount* podcast is so fun and a really great listen. I was so honoured when the guys asked me to be a guest – and I was completely touched and flattered when they asked me to write this foreword. It's so incredible to be part of this book!

I am so happy for the guys and so proud of how far they have come and where *Four Finger Discount* has taken them. They deserve all the recognition and praise. They ask the right questions and really show their passion for this production. I have had such a great time watching their endeavours grow. Their expertise and fervour for this show really shines through on the pages of this book. Whether you are new to the show or a long-time fan, this guide has something for everyone. This book will give you so much insight and knowledge about the episodes and what this production is about. These two have really done a marvellous job at writing the supreme *Simpsons* guide for fans out there. They capture the love and spirit of the show and serve it up to you in a fun and enjoyable read!

Nikki Isordia

Contents

Contents

Contents

Welcome to *Homer's Odyssey*

Welcome to Four Finger Discount's guide to *The Simpsons*! Congratulations on your excellent decision to purchase this book. It is, undoubtedly, one of the few sound investments you could have made in these troubled times. Presuming you did buy it, of course, and aren't just standing in a bookstore idly leafing through pages for what by now has already started to feel like a little bit too long. You can feel the eyes upon you, the silent indignation from the staff that screams 'This isn't a library!' Guiltily, you put the book back, and are no longer reading this.

OK, now that those guys are gone, we can get stuck in. We don't like to give away the good stuff for free! Well, technically that's not true. See, for those unaware, Four Finger Discount is a free weekly podcast devoted to all things *Simpsons*. Each week we bring our take on the show to millions* of people across the world. Having spent the best part of three years bringing auditory enjoyment, we're here to give your visual ears† just the same amount of fun!

The idea behind this book is to explore the unique impact that *The Simpsons* had on our lives, and on the

* Thousands
† Eyes

1

lives of our generation from all over the world. Through a collection of conversations about individual seasons, specific breakdowns of the episodes that had a big impact on us as fans of the show, our favourite guest stars and exclusive interviews, we'll be trying to remind you of a time when *The Simpsons* was the most important show on television. Everybody who is a *Simpsons* fan will have their own favourite episodes, quotes they still use every day, and memories of watching the show when they were younger. We hope that by reading about ours, it will remind you of yours. Essentially, if you're feeling a little melancholy and your doctor has prescribed a big ol' dose of nostalgia, then consider your script filled.

We'll also be throwing in the ultimate trivia challenge for diehard fans and exclusives from behind the scenes. We've got it all! Well . . . apart from moving pictures, or a touch screen, or sound, or a level-up progression system, or anything else the kids are addicted to these days. Frankly it's a wonder that this dying medium* is still around at all. Oh well . . . enjoy.

---

* Our publishers object to the term 'dying medium' and would prefer we substitute it with 'relevancy-challenged entertainment product' – Cheerfully withdrawn.

What *The Simpsons* Means to Me – Mitch

'Did you watch *The Simpsons* last night?'

Growing up in the 90s, there was no single more important question that you could get asked at school on any given day. What is Pythagoras' theorem? What is Newton's Second Law? Where is your homework? – None of those questions would have as much bearing on your future as your ability to wax lyrical about Homer and Bart's antics on TV the night before. That was the question that would drive and define friendships, and has had more importance in my life than trigonometry ever will.

I fondly remember chatting with my childhood friends, Tom, Sam and Josh about what episodes had aired the night before. I went to school with Josh, and played cricket with Sam and Tom, so it often meant the same episode would be recapped two or three times in one day. The same lines, the same jokes, but always the same amount of laughter. Beyond childhood friendships, it gave me a great way to be able to enjoy something with my dad. We would both hustle through the supermarket on weekly shopping trips to make sure we made it back by 6 p.m. Later, he would make the executive decision that the shopping be rescheduled to whatever time of the week *Desperate Housewives* was on. It was one of the first shows we could watch together and both enjoy, even if for different reasons. The show had a brilliant ability to aim both high and low with the same joke. For example, Homer suggestively talking about how much fun could be had in bed whilst imagining eating a big sandwich. I was too young to understand the sexual connotation, but I would laugh because it looked funny, Dad would laugh at the same time for the more adult reasons, and for a beautiful moment, it felt like we were on the same level.

One could argue that the 90s were a golden age for mass consumption of TV serials and sitcoms. Before streaming and on-demand access changed the scene, we were all forced into experiencing shows at the same time. It also coincided with a time of increasing popularity of American shows on foreign TV. It created a perfect storm for shows like *Seinfeld*, *Friends*, *Home Improvement*, *Roseanne*, and of course, *The Simpsons*. It made for many great 'event' moments of television. Gathering friends together in October to watch the 'Treehouse of Horror' specials on video was an annual tradition in Australia well before anybody was going out trick-or-treating. Around this time, another cultural phenomenon was around the corner: a little thing called the internet. There's not much that makes me feel old, but remembering a time *before* Google certainly does. In its infancy, we didn't realise the incredible connective power that would soon be bestowed upon us.

Today, the television world is in a very different landscape. In the age of streaming content at your leisure, very few people are watching anything at the same time. Rather than seek out conversations about TV with

like-minded friends, I almost have to avoid them in fear
of them being further ahead than I am. I still haven't
forgiven my groomsman, Michael, for spoiling the first
season of *Dexter* when I was only two episodes in. So,
conversations about TV today tend to be more along
these lines:

'Did you watch *House of Cards* last night?'

'Yeah, I did.'

'Oh, how sad was it when Doug got—'

'Wait! I only watched three episodes, how much did
you watch?'

'Oh! Wow. I've already watched the whole season
three times and read every forum about the finale.'

'Right . . . Sorry, what were you about to say about
Doug?'

'. . . Never mind.'

'Did something bad happen?'

'We'll talk in a month.'

So, where does that leave *The Simpsons*? The show
now exists in a vacuum; locked in a beautiful time and
space known as nostalgia, where there are no spoilers
and everybody knows your name. When we started our
podcast, Four Finger Discount, we wanted to try and
recreate the shared experience of watching a TV show
together. Not in the same room. But together. We had
no idea that so many around the world wanted to come
along for the ride. I've always said that *The Simpsons*
was the sort of show that offered one thing for kids, and
another for adults. It's now been good enough to offer
me a third level of enjoyment as I get to engage with
people all over the world on a weekly basis. At their
core, these conversations aren't *about The Simpsons*,

despite the content. They're about connecting with people. More so than any medium, great TV shows can unite audiences and create friendships.

Many words have been written about *The Simpsons* in the decades since it first graced the airwaves. But, hopefully, none like what you are about to read. *The Simpsons* has transcended television in a way that very few shows ever do. It's a show that doesn't have fans so much as followers. Millions of them around the world. Followers who for the best of their formative years honed their worldview through a yellow prism. Followers who were getting a lesson in comedy, morals, emotion, love and absurdity each night at 6 p.m. This book is as much about remembering how great that felt as it is about analysing the show itself. We hope that by sharing some of our stories, it will rekindle some special memories from your own childhood spent growing up on the same stuff we did, no matter what your background is.

It can't be overstated how important the show has been to the entertainment that we currently enjoy. Virtually all modern animated comedy owes a debt to *The Simpsons*. Thanks to its influence over its fanbase, what started as a counterculture show eventually became culture itself. Sometimes satire can lag behind the changing times and becomes irrelevant. Sometimes it remains relevant for so long that it eventually becomes the truth. In the case of *The Simpsons*, satire forced a change in the direction that the truth was going to go. *The Simpsons* lasted so long that the shows and families they once lampooned died off, and new shows and families sprung up in their shadow. Only this time, rather than look to differentiate themselves from the rebel new-comer, they were trying to live up to their image. Were it not for asking 'Did you watch *The Simpsons* last night?' I'd never have gone on to ask, 'Did you see *South Park* last night?'

I really hope you enjoy our book. It's written by fans, for fans. But it's also written for my dad, and my mum, and for my friends. And for your friends, and your mums and dads and whoever else this show brought you closer to. I hope we can take you back to those special moments in your life that made you connect with the show, and I hope one day you get to share them with Dando and me. If you ever do, you'll know how to start the conversation.

So, did you watch *The Simpsons* last night?

What *The Simpsons* Means to Me – Dando

Is *The Simpsons* the greatest show of all time? Maybe. Is it my favourite show of all time? Most certainly.

For listeners of our podcast, it's no secret that I was a late bloomer when it comes to being a *Simpsons* fan. In fact, I wasn't allowed to watch the show until 1995 when my mother's '*Simpsons* ban' was finally lifted. Why was I banned? I'll get into that in a moment.

I can still remember the first time I ever saw *The Simpsons*. It was a commercial for 'Bart the Genius' that aired during a syndicated episode of *The Muppet Show* on Channel 10, which for Australian viewers was the home of *The Simpsons* for over 20 years – 6 p.m. weeknights became an institution for all of us wanting our fix of *The Simpsons*, which would air in direct competition to the national news programmes on the opposing commercial stations. To me, *The Simpsons* was the single greatest investment Channel 10 ever made.

Once Australian Pay TV provider Foxtel launched in the mid-to-late 90s, the 6 p.m. weeknight Simpsons ritual that my sister Stacey and I had was then trumped by the 'Super Simpsons Weekends', where FOX8 would air back-to-back *Simpsons* episodes for three hours every Saturday and Sunday morning. As a fan you honestly couldn't ask for much more. In their infancy Foxtel even used Bart Simpson as their mascot. His slogan of 'I want my Foxtel!' worked a charm, as it was all I needed to hear to make me beg my parents to start throwing their money away, just so I could cram in 10 more hours of *Simpsons* reruns each week.

There's just something about the show that taps into the memory of simpler times, when all you had to worry about was what Mum was cooking for dinner, whether wrestling was real or fake, and whether or not you'd remembered to feed your Tamagotchi that day. One of my favourite memories watching the show is Stacey and I trying to solve the mystery of who shot Mr. Burns, or when FOX8 aired the 'Simpsons Fan-fest', a 24/7 Simpsons marathon that aired in conjunction with the Sydney 2000 Olympics. Whilst millions of Australians watched the legendary Cathy Freeman win gold in the 400m sprint, I was spending a good portion of my school holidays staying up late through the night and recording *The Simpsons*, ensuring I cut out all of the ad breaks. Despite now owning the DVDs, I still have some of those tapes, probably because I can't bring myself to throw them out when I think of how many man hours went into making them.

In regard to why I was originally banned from watching the show, it's a simple story really. The year was 1992 and four-year-old Dando was watching the original 'Treehouse of Horror' special. During the segment 'Bad Dream House' I apparently thought it would be fine to imitate the Simpson family by getting a knife from the kitchen drawer and pacing back into the lounge. Mum was not amused, but can you blame her? I'm lucky I wasn't committed.

As a result, I was forced into years of having to sit and

listen as all my school friends discussed what they saw on *The Simpsons* the night prior, trying to piece together my own version of the show in my mind. Much like Bart in 'The Itchy & Scratchy Movie', I'd try and find ways to watch the show without Mum knowing. The obvious option being to go to my friends' houses and watch – however just like Homer, Mum had already told their parents of the infamous ban.

Looking back, I'm glad that all happened. Not the knife-wielding, but the ban in general. During those few years of *Simpsons* withdrawals I developed such a strong desire to watch the show that when the time finally came, I loved it more than I think I would have if I'd always had access to it. Amazingly, it exceeded all expectations of what I had envisioned this phenomenon to be.

The Simpsons connects with me on several levels. Hidden throughout the timeless one-liners and sight gags are themes that now play a key role in my day-to-day life. 'Lisa the Vegetarian' taught me tolerance and acceptance, Mr. Bergstrom showed me it's important to believe in myself, then there's the ending of 'Lisa on Ice', a moment that leaves me fighting back tears almost every time I watch it.

The magic of the show is that as I grow older I can start to appreciate it for different reasons. Bart's anti-authority antics were appealing to me as a child, then throughout my teenage years I matured and realised I was more like Lisa. Now that I'm 29 and married, the relationship between Homer and Marge is something I can truly understand. Like all good marriages, they love, they fight, they enjoy different things, but through it all they remain best friends.

Sentimentality aside, it must be said that at its core *The Simpsons* succeeds because it is just so damn entertaining. It says something about the calibre of the writing when people still quote a line that aired 25 years ago as if it were written only yesterday. In fact many of the gags from the earlier seasons are just as topical today as they were two decades ago.

This is a show that can unite strangers and help forge friendships with people you've nothing in common with outside of the ability to recite 'The Monorail Song'. Its characters and stories are so relatable that more often than not I find myself saying, 'It's like that time when (insert Simpsons moment)', comparing a wacky Simpsons scenario to something that just happened in my day. This underlying ability to relate with its audience has been the backbone of what's kept *The Simpsons* so successful. Even now, as I write this, I'm picturing a thousand monkeys at a thousand typewriters and wondering which of us is doing a better job.

With the development of the internet and social media, the show has managed to find a new lease on life, becoming the conduit for social satire of major global events. A simple *Simpsons* screenshot captioned with its relevance to a news story is all a user needs to generate engagement with their post, a tactic we are now seeing used more frequently by even the most reputable of news sources. After all, the Simpsons have done everything, right?

If you're reading this then chances are we both have a lot in common. You didn't just watch *The Simpsons*, you lived it. In your circle of friends, you're 'the *Simpsons* guy/girl', the one they think of whenever they see or hear the show, forever tagging you in *Simpsons*-related posts on social media. Four Finger Discount was born with the intent to find and connect with fans such as yourself, creating a global forum where we could engage and discuss what the show means to us all. I look forward to hearing from you and hope you enjoy our book.

Season 1 (1989-90)
In Conversation

MITCH: Season 1 has almost become the forgotten season. It very rarely gets any airplay on TV these days, I guess due to the animation being so different. That said, I've always felt like fixating on the look of the series and writing it off is missing the forest for the trees. If you can look beyond the animation and the slightly different vocal performances, there's some great stuff to be had.

DANDO: To be perfectly honest, the first season isn't one I visit too regularly. Mostly for those reasons of it being a little less accessible on TV these days. That said, it does have some great moments, like Homer's (bad) advice on handling a bully by going for the family jewels in 'Bart the General', or Marge supporting Lisa through her depression in 'Moaning Lisa'. However, since the episodes aired in a different order to which they were produced, it can get a little jarring at times. A prime example of this being 'There's No Disgrace Like Home', where Lisa is essentially just another 'Bart' as she misbehaves at the power plant family picnic. Thankfully it didn't take the writers long to realise she needed her own identity.

M: I think TV writing has come a long way since then, but at that time it was common for sitcom characters to evolve throughout the early episodes, or even across the first few seasons. George Costanza from *Seinfeld* is

15

almost unrecognisable from Season 1 to Season 4. You also have to factor in how much lead time was involved in making an episode. I get the feeling that by the time they knew who the characters were, several episodes were already in the can.

D: The first few episodes may be uneven, but it really didn't take very long for the series to find its stride. By the time they got to 'The Telltale Head' all of the characters were locked down. From there they moved on to 'Life on the Fast Lane', which is stunningly good for being only the eighth episode of a series.

M: I nearly hold that one up in my top 10 all-time episodes. I love the way they explore Marge's doubt in her marriage at a time when so many female characters in sitcoms were married to schlubs and never really got to voice an opinion. It also gives us a decent serving of Albert Brooks as bowling Lothario, Jacques.

D: Interestingly, that was Albert's second time working on the show.

M: Exactly! That was something that had snuck past me before, but *The Simpsons'* relationship with Albert Brooks began with a cameo as RV Bob in 'The Call of the Simpsons'. It gave a taste as to how much comedic energy he could put into a character that, on rewatching, left me craving more.

D: His sales pitch of the camper is one of the greatest of all time.

M: It has its own satellite! For mine, 'The Call of the Simpsons' is the best early example of the show pitching comedy at both young and old audiences. While the adults were laughing at Homer getting declined for a loan, kids were laughing at him haplessly wrestling critters or being mistaken for Bigfoot.

D: Just kids?

M: OK, adults laughed at that, too.

D: As absurd as 'The Call of The Simpsons' is, it's just so much fun. It was the first time the series used their capacity as a cartoon to push the boundaries of what was possible for a scripted comedy in prime-time.

M: It really helped set them apart, didn't it?

D: Exactly. Real-life sitcoms couldn't have a baby join a family of bears, or launch a rabbit through the air with a trap gone wrong. Those events would be a bridge too far for almost any other series at the time, but for *The Simpsons* they would prove to only be the tip of the iceberg.

M: Another thing that set the show apart from the outset was its willingness to tackle adult issues. Whether that was a way to guard against the perception of being for children, I don't know, but it's a surprise to go back and see early episodes dealing with adultery, depression, suicide, bullying and alcoholism head on.

D: I was amazed by that as well. For a show in its infancy, it's a brave move to tackle those dark themes, even though I felt they may have taken it a little too far in 'Homer's Odyssey' when Homer was prepared to jump off a bridge. Homer wanting to end his life because he was embarrassed about being unemployed felt unrealistic, and doesn't set the best example for younger viewers. On the other hand, 'Moaning Lisa' taught us all a great lesson that it's OK to feel down from time to time. Marge's advice to Lisa, 'Always be yourself. You want to be sad? Be sad. We'll ride it out with you', is some of the best parenting you'll ever see on a television programme.

M: From the outset, it was clear that there were deeper stories trying to be told than the overlying comedy would suggest, and frankly the writing was so good that it felt perfectly natural. You mentioned Homer

17

wanting to jump off a bridge, and you're right that it's a very dark moment, especially watching him write out a suicide note, but the show was always able to find gallows humour in those situations. Case in point: when Homer stops to oil a squeaky fence as he leaves his yard, it's a brilliant joke about Homer missing the point of a situation. He's about to walk out on everything, but still sees that as his duty. He also drags that huge boulder all the way to the bridge, only to find an identical one already there. Those moments keep the show from becoming too dark, and are reflective of the early pacing of the comedy. The downtime in between the jokes typically served to make the laughs hit harder.

D: I've always felt that the season finale 'Some Enchanted Evening', which was originally intended to be the pilot, comes across like an extended version of an earlier Ullman short. It makes sense, given that it was the first episode produced, however due to some animation issues they had to bring in David Silverman to essentially remake the episode, meaning it was pushed back to the end of the season. Opting to go with 'Simpsons Roasting on an Open Fire' instead was either a stroke of luck or a stroke of genius, or both, as it really set the tone for the show. Heartfelt, family-based storytelling was the foundation for the series in its earlier years, and this episode delivers that in spades.

M: Despite one or two missteps, it's striking how much the show had already found its feet within the first dozen episodes. Considering it's only the second episode of the series, 'Bart the Genius' is about as polished as Season 1 gets. Aside from expected animation differences, this episode could slot into the second season with ease, particularly from a writing standpoint. Bart's character is given real depth as he struggles to deal with the results of him cheating on the aptitude test, showing that behind his mask of mischief hides a 10-year-old boy searching for approval.

D: Of all the characters introduced this season, Bart was certainly one that the writers seemed to fully grasp from the outset.

M: I really prefer this early version of Bart as he still has a vulnerability to him. I feel like over time as he became convinced he could get away with anything, he occasionally gets a little too cocksure. Watching Bart squirm a little bit from time to time gives his rebellious nature the extra edge of a high-wire act that could come crashing down at any moment.

D: It also helps him earn some sympathy. When he is sent to France to essentially work as a slave on a foreign exchange programme, you feel so bad for the kid that you can't help but forgive him when he acts out in other episodes.

M: Overall, if you wanted to go back and watch Season 1, your enjoyment would depend a bit on where you set your expectations.

D: Yeah, you can't expect it to be what you came to love in Season 6, for example, but to understand where the show is you need to go and see where it came from.

M: I think you could put the first four episodes in their own basket where it almost feels like the writers broke into four different groups and produced their own episodes, such is the difference in characters from one to the next, but from that point on, it feels like watching a 90% complete as we remember it show. Sideshow Bob, for example, is presented exactly as he would go on to be remembered.

D: There really is a huge amount to enjoy. As somebody who didn't get to watch it as a kid, I was surprised by how much I enjoyed going back through each episode. I'd certainly recommend them to anybody who hasn't watched them, if for nothing more than to get a better understanding of the show.

'Life on the Fast Lane'
(Season 1, Episode 9)
Review by Mitch

Having forgotten Marge's birthday, Homer rushes out to buy her a gift. His choice, a bowling ball with his own named inscribed (so she would know it was from him) leaves a lot to be desired. His plan backfires when Marge starts bowling out of spite, and meets Lothario of the lanes, Jacques. As Jacques pulls out all the moves, Marge's commitment to her marriage is put to the ultimate test.

'Life on the Fast Lane' is the first Marge-centric episode of *The Simpsons*, but is remembered more for a tour-de-force performance from Albert Brooks. Albert had already guested on the show previously, playing RV Salesman Cowboy Bob in 'The Call of the Simpsons', but where he had only played a cameo in that role, here he plays his first of many memorable guest characters who are central to the plot. As something of a coming of age moment, 'Life on the Fast Lane' was the first episode to win a Prime-time Emmy award for Outstanding Animated Program.

I'd be lying if I said that I had this as a favourite when I was growing up. It is one of the least child-friendly episodes of the first season as it features very little of Bart, focuses on themes such as love and infidelity, and has very few *cartoon* moments to keep young minds interested. Looking back on it now as a married man, it strikes (hehe) an emotional chord. I also have a far greater understanding of the comedy. Anything from the first season can be difficult to come across on television now, as networks try to avoid the jarring visuals, but if you have the means and haven't watched this one for a while, you'd be doing yourself a disservice if you didn't track it down.

For the first time, the character of Marge is really fleshed out. Up until now she had mostly been a side-player to the more marketable Simpsons members. Whilst she had her moments, such as her brilliant speech to Lisa that she'll do the smiling for both of them in 'Moaning Lisa', she had never really had any defined purpose of her own outside of reacting to those around her. If the kids were sad she would comfort them. If Homer had something on his mind she would lend him her ear. But what of her own feelings beyond those that are expected of a wife and mother? It's fulfilling to see her fleshed out and driving her own story for a change.

Watching Homer and Marge simply discussing things in bed is one of the great joys of the James L. Brooks years. They are presented in a voyeuristic way that would put producers of *Big Brother* or *Gogglebox* to shame. The connection between husband and wife had a greater prominence in relation to the plot, as the events of the day would have a real impact on the two. This helped establish the Simpsons as real beings – entities to care about, not just to be laughed at. It's genuinely painful to watch just how *real* Homer is as he begins to fear that he has lost his connection to Marge. Your heart breaks for the guy as he realises that his selfishness might have pushed his wife away, to the point that he can't even bring it up with her for fear of what the answer might be . . .

The answer that he doesn't want to hear comes in the form of Albert Brooks's Jacques. Legend has it that for his performance Albert improvised close to three hours of dialogue that hit the cutting room floor, and often scenes where Marge laughs at Jacques were unscripted bouts of laughter from Julie Kavner, unable to control herself. If there was any table-read in history that I could insert myself into, this would be right up there, but I'd settle for any day that Albert happened by the building. His ability to *create* funny lines that aren't necessarily jokes is unparalleled. Whether explaining that brunch comes with a slice of cantaloupe at the end, or screaming out for four onion rings, he has such a hyper-intensity as an actor that virtually every character he has played has gone down in history as a fan-favourite.

As much as *The Simpsons* would push the envelope, there were certain boundaries that were unlikely to be crossed, and Marge actually going through with an affair is one of them. Just as Homer would come to a sudden realisation and snap out of temptation in 'The Last Temptation of Homer', Marge comes to her senses at just the right time. While it's a theme that has been revisited, it has never been bettered. For a good three years, I couldn't leave a room without declaring 'I'm going to the back-seat of my car with the woman I love, and I won't be back for TEN minutes!'

A shining light from the first season, 'Life on the Fast Lane' sees the show really making its mark. In the same way 'Marge vs. the Monorail' defined the Conan O'Brien years. 'Life' is a textbook example of James L. Brooks at his best.

What did we learn?

To make a 7–10 split, tell them the 8 pin is a cop.

'Krusty Gets Busted'
(Season 1, Episode 12)
Review by Dando

After Homer witnesses a shoplifting, he identifies the culprit as being Krusty the Clown. Devastated by the news, Bart refuses to believe that Krusty could possibly be guilty. Teaming up with Lisa, he sets out to uncover the true culprit: Sideshow Bob.

The first season of *The Simpsons* can sometimes be looked upon rather harshly by critics. Not only do the characters look and sound different, they also tend to behave in ways that don't stay true to who they are from Season 2 onward. These things never really bothered me, for I've always considered these 13 episodes as living within their own universe, designed to build a solid foundation for success in future seasons. The ingredients were all there, they just needed to be stirred a little more. There's no denying that 'Krusty Gets Busted' is guilty of the occasional continuity error (Krusty getting excited about pork, Lou is white, etc.), however the way it manages to establish the series' most iconic villain so flawlessly is a victory that can't be denied.

Whilst writers Jay Kogen and Wallace Wolodarsky deserve credit for such a tight script, which actually started out at a whopping 78 pages long, the episode's ability to stand above the other 12 of Season 1 can be attributed to another two men in particular, the first being director Brad Bird. Much as in 'Like Father, Like Clown', Bird's directing expertise is on full show as we feel like we are watching a film, as opposed to an upstart cartoon still finding its feet. Whether it's the way he chose to begin each act with a close-up (Krusty's banner, Krusty behind bars and then Sideshow Bob's poster), or the classic 'big shoes to fill' revelation, it's no surprise Bird went on to even bigger success in Hollywood.

The other man in question is Sideshow Bob himself, Kelsey Grammer, whose voice acting and singing talents are a thing of beauty in this story's final act as he busts out his own rendition of Cole Porter's 'Ev'ry Time We Say Goodbye'. In fact, it was after hearing Grammer regularly sing Tony Bennett songs on the set of *Cheers* that Sam Simon (a former writer on the show) decided he was the man for the role. With Grammer bringing the pompous flair for theatrics that audiences had grown accustomed to seeing in Frasier Crane, this proved to be yet another casting masterstroke from Simon. In an era when Smithers was black and Homer forgot he wasn't Walter Matthau, Sideshow Bob immediately 'feels' like Sideshow Bob from the moment we hear him speak, which in itself was a moment of directing genius . . .

For the first two thirds of the episode, Sideshow Bob lurks in the shadows, merely communicating with viewers by saddened facial expressions as his illiterate boss fires him from a cannon. It's not until Krusty is found guilty and Bob is handed the reins to the show that we are fully introduced to this complex criminal mastermind. Contrary to what you'd expect from a wacky sidekick on a children's afternoon show hosted by a clown, Bob is a learned man with acquired tastes and a thirst for providing his own vision of quality programming, which apparently still requires him to parade around semi-nude in a green skirt.

Perhaps the most interesting aspect of it all is that even after Bob's evil plot is foiled by his 'big, ugly feet', it can't be denied that his version of the show is actually far superior to Krusty's. He offered young viewers an opportunity to learn, read classic novels like *The Man in the Iron Mask*, as well as discuss their problems on segments such as the hilariously delivered, *Choices*, a far cry from Krusty's tendency to encourage children to make reference to the idea of killing themselves. I know it's only a cartoon, but that moment makes me cringe every time. Whilst Bob's actions in framing Krusty were reprehensible, his motives were genuine and were having a positive impact on his audience. Even as he is being hauled away in a police van, his final words of freedom are a plea for adults to 'treat kids as equals. They're people, too!' Despite this, the right man (eventually) came out on top.

Krusty may have his faults, but nobody deserves the injustice he receives as Springfield once again falls into the trap of mob mentality, burning Krusty merchandise à la the burning of Beatles records in the 1960s. When everyone had given up on Krusty, including his loyal fanbase, Bart's determination to not join the 'winning team' and instead defend his hero is truly admirable. When Krusty looks him straight in the eye and says 'I didn't do it', he sees an innocent man; now he just has to find a way to prove it. The 'I didn't do it' line was a nice throwback to Krusty's catchphrase in the opening scene, but what I love more is how it was used once again as an homage in Season 5's 'Bart Gets Famous'.

This episode serves not only as an introduction to one of the series' main anarchists, but also one of its most infamous rivalries. It gave the writers a reason to continue to bring back Sideshow Bob as he attempts to exact revenge on Bart, resulting in some of the most golden moments of the show. Without 'Krusty Gets Busted' there'd be no classic retelling of *HMS Pinafore*, no cousin Merl, but most importantly, there'd be no rakes.

What did we learn?

Heavily salted snack treats make for a perfect hideaway from armed robbery.

An Interview with David Silverman

David Silverman has been involved with The Simpsons *from the very beginning, animating the shorts for* The Tracey Ullman Show. *His influence over the look and feel of the show can't be overstated. He is responsible for many of the animation rules for the characters, and is frequently the man behind difficult animation sequences. One of the greatest examples of his work is Homer's hallucination in 'El Viaje Misterioso de Nuestro Jomer (The Mysterious Voyage of Homer)'. He continues to exert influence over the show as a mentor to the current animation team, and is a true legend in his field. He took some time out one evening to discuss his, and the show's legacy.*

How does it feel to have created an icon?
It's a funny thing because from my point of view it's hard to see it. I mean I know I'm one of the people who helped create the show but that's not something I ever think about. When I was a student at UCLA, I wouldn't say it was a *goal* per se but I remember thinking how nice it'd be to have the opportunity to be involved with a great animated film or television show. You know, to be a part of creating an animation that really meant something to people. I guess I can check that off my list of goals I've apparently now completed.

When was the first moment you realised that The Simpsons *was going to be a huge success*?
There's actually a funny story to that. I remember when the first episode aired we had a really great bowling party with everyone, but there was no merchandising at that time since we were only just starting. What we did get though were these *Simpsons* crew Letterman jackets which were fashionable back then, they were black with red leather sleeves and had all our names embroidered on them. On the back they featured the iconic image that I drew that has the family all waving, with Bart in the middle using his slingshot. I remember getting notes over the phone from Matt Groening and Sam Simon telling me what they wanted that image to look like, so I drew it all pretty fast. It's rather crude and I remember at one point Wes Archer cleaned it up, but then Matt and Sam said they'd rather stick with the older crude version since it had a fun energy to itself.

Anyway, I grew up in Silver Springs, Maryland just outside of Washington DC and I'd gone back home to visit my family for Christmas. So I was walking around the shopping mall as you normally do at Christmas time and people start stopping me and saying 'Hey David!' and at first I'm thinking is this an old friend or someone I went to school with that I don't remember? However, it turns out that they didn't know me, they just read my name on my jacket and wanted to ask where they could buy one for themselves. So I had to explain to them that I worked on the show and they were only a gift for the crew. After that I distinctly remember looking over the mall map trying to find a certain store and overheard someone behind me say to his friend, 'Hey did you see that *Simpsons* Christmas special? It was really cool man, really funny', and I'm thinking, 'Wow, we've only aired one episode and people are already talking about the show!' For two years I'd never heard anyone talking about the Tracey Ullman shorts, but suddenly everyone seemed to know about *The Simpsons*.

Once more episodes aired, the show became this massive hit and we couldn't believe it. We were all just so busy. Personally, I was involved with five episodes in the first season, directing four and sort of re-directing 'Some Enchanted Evening'. Then as a few years went by and we reached Season 3, I was finally able to sit back and smell the roses a little bit.

What exactly went wrong with 'Some Enchanted Evening'?
Well we had someone assigned to direct it and he was a very good guy, but he didn't really embrace what was happening on the show. It was really interesting, he was a bit older than Wes and me and had been in the business a lot longer, around ten years or so, actually – maybe it was less but he just came across like a guy with a lot of experience. He had a crew that he brought in who had worked on *Mighty Mouse* and they all had a different attitude to the rest of us. They had this attitude that they were the new stars here, so they didn't really endear themselves to me, but I was taking it in my stride, I didn't have time to deal with any nonsense anyhow.

So, they gave this guy the first episode because he had experience directing half-hour animation, and by 'they' I mean the people at Klasky-Csupo. Gracie Films didn't really know what was going on in terms of the animation at that point in time. Now, I'd read the script and envisioned it in my head, but when I saw the way this guy and his team were approaching it, I was thinking that these aren't the characters I remember Wes and I working on during the Tracey Ullman days. You know, you look at the very last handful of Tracey Ullman shorts, they're not as crude as everyone seems to remember them as. The first ones were, because we were still figuring it out as we were going along, but by the time you start getting around the midpoint, around episode 20, the animation starts becoming a lot more refined. In fact, the last ten are pretty much what the characters look like because Wes and I based our model sheets on what we'd been doing at the end of our Tracey Ullman run. So, we had a sense of dimensionality and the way the characters acted.

As far as cartoons are concerned, they were much more grounded, weren't they?
There was a sort of underplayed approach to their performance that would result in more natural, calmed-down acting as opposed to what I call cartoon vaudeville where everything's a big joke. It's not a bad style, but it just didn't fit this show's sense of humour like it would for a show such as *Ren & Stimpy*. Those shows are essentially telling a different set of jokes, but if you start doing that with *The Simpsons* it doesn't make any sense because there's more of a reality. That's what's funny about it, they're these funny-looking characters acting human-like and that's something I had a tough time communicating to the original director. Jumping forward, I guess that may be why they made me supervising director, since they liked my sense of taste.

Did he take any of your advice on board?
He still did it his way and I thought 'Well, I don't have time to worry about it because I have my own episodes to finish.' Plus, I wasn't in charge at that point, anyway. However, when it came back it was quite literally a disaster. I wasn't at the initial screening but I heard about it. At first, they were laughing because of the thrill of seeing these characters all moving onscreen and whatnot, and then it got real quiet to the point where by the end there was not one laugh. Not one. Jim Brooks got very dour and sour looking and did not move at all. He basically said we couldn't air it because it's just not going to work. So, then it became nail-biting for me because they said 'Well, we're waiting for David's show ('Bart the Genius') and *he* worked on the shorts, so if his show doesn't work then we'll just pull the plug on the whole thing.' Now *that* put a lot of pressure on me. I mean, I thought I'd got it right, since I animated a lot of it here, which we still do today. A lot of people think it's all animated in Korea, but it's really not, it's done here and just gets cleaned up in Korea.

So, how did you feel when you first screened your episode?
I had confidence in what I'd done but I wasn't sure they were going to like it, so I just hoped and waited to see what happened. For the first time ever, everybody turned up to the studio for the screening, which I don't think has ever happened since, I know Jim hasn't ever been back. So they're all watching the episode and everyone laughed from the very beginning. I'd forgotten that I'd added in a joke late in the process, the shot where

Maggie spells out E=MC with the building blocks. The other director didn't seem to enhance his episode, he almost had a feeling of contempt for the script. I think he was unaware of the way things were working here. The annoying thing was that when I re-directed it I was only allowed to fix around 70% of it, so some scenes still look a little weird, but we just didn't have the money to be able to fix the whole thing.

When we were rewatching these episodes, we both felt 'Bart the Genius' really stood out from both a writing and animation point of view.

Jon Vitti wrote such a great script for that, I remember reading it and thinking this is the funniest thing ever written for animation. In 1989 there hadn't been a lot of hilarious animated features – I mean I love *Pinocchio* and *Snow White*, but they're not hilarious by any means. It was as funny as any Warner Bros short that I had seen, perhaps funnier because it's a half hour of sustained comedy and I'd never seen that before in animation. I like *The Flintstones* but I can't tell you about a *Flintstones* episode that I'm dying to watch again because I was laughing the whole way through or it was visually stimulating. I recognised that there had been no half-hour animation like this before and as a director I wanted to make sure I got out of the way of the funny material. Don't kill the jokes, just deliver the goods. I remember thinking 'Don't screw this up, don't kill the timing!' I'd been watching people like Chaplin since I was five, so hopefully that taught me a thing or two.

Do you have a favourite emotional scene that you animated?

I remember I always thought the animation was really solid in 'Bart Gets An F' – it may not have a lot of laughs but it's got some really great animation. Like the scene where Bart's crying, I realised it was better to have him cover his face with his paper, it was a real emotional way to present him as upset. When people are crying in public they hide their face, it's just a natural response because they don't want people to see them like that. You still get the same emotional impact and it was a little less distressing than watching Bart with his face scrunched up. A lot of thought went into that scene.

What excites you about your job now compared to back when you were directing the Tracey Ullman shorts and earlier episodes?

You know, it's almost the same thing, but what I enjoy is getting involved with very detailed drawing. It doesn't have to be a whole sequence, it might just be a little prop or something. Sometimes I like to just get involved with a whole new thing – even as we speak I'm working on co-writing a script, which is something I've never done before. I came up with an idea and Al Jean wanted me to co-write it with a very talented writer Brian Kelley, who was for some reason very jovial about writing it with me. Whether it's directing, writing or whatever I always continue to count my good fortunes, however I probably don't do as much animation now as I'd like to. Part of it just being too busy with other things, and the other part being that we now have so many great animators working on the show. That's not to say that we didn't use to have great animators, we just have a lot more of them now. There was a time when we couldn't compete with companies like Disney, but now we have a lot of ex-Disney animators coming to work on *The Simpsons* because Disney isn't doing traditional 2D animation any more. Many have now moved into CG, but a lot of them say they just got tired of not drawing anymore. I mean we have an incredible ex-Disney/Dreamworks animator who I've known for many years named Kathy Zielinski, who was just at the studio one day and I had no idea she'd been hired. It's amazing to get the chance to work with so many talented people, they're all remarkable.

The animation style of* The Simpsons *has changed so much over the last 30 years, do you prefer the old pen to paper method or the digital techniques that get used today?
It depends. I love working on pen and paper but at the same time I also really like the capabilities of what we can accomplish nowadays due to the technology we have. There's some aspects of the old pen method that are really satisfying I do miss, but there's positives in everything and what we can achieve now from an animation perspective is incredible.

Matt Schofield credits the animation sequence in 'Homie the Clown' where Homer and Krusty ride the mini-cycle as inspiring him to one day work on the show. How does it feel working with people who you inspired?

Wow, I didn't know that! That's pretty awesome, isn't it? You know, I forget that I've been here a lot longer than a lot of the animators that we have now, I guess I never really think that they look up to me to an extent. That definitely makes me feel pretty special.

You've credited Brad Bird as one of your biggest influences: what were you able to learn and apply from your time working with him on the show?
In the beginning I was very inspired by Brad Bird's 'Krusty Gets Busted'. I learned so much from Brad; in particular he gave me a much better understanding of what can be achieved directorially. It was like a crash course in directing, he's just so passionate and had so many smart ideas about what we could all do with our episodes. He was always thinking of new ways to approach something and had such a boundless energy that was so inspiring. If we were ever stuck on something we'd always ask 'What would Brad do?' He taught us to really get into what the story was about, making sure the staging predicated what the storytelling was about, finding the best way to stage a shot so that it supported the story but didn't undermine it. He was always very gracious and applauded you when you did great work, which was an inspiring trait that I tried to carry over with me when working with my staff.

What was the first animation sequence on The Simpsons *that made you genuinely excited?*
I'd have to say the scene in the very first episode that I directed, 'Bart the Genius', when Homer is chasing Bart through the house and banging on his bedroom door. I

also directed the train dream sequence when Bart is trying to solve a math equation and gets overwhelmed by his imagination.

'The Longest Daycare' is absolutely brilliant. Which Simpsons character would you love to star in your next short film?
That was a lot of fun because I did a lot of material with stuff I came up with myself – in particular I loved animating the scene where the caterpillar is crawling along Maggie's shoulder. If I was going to do another one of those I think I'd want it to star Homer, a pantomime with Homer would be a lot of fun. Everyone is used to Maggie not speaking, so doing one with a conventional character like Homer would be a great challenge, if I ever get the time!

Was there ever a piece of animation you wished you could go back and tweak?
I'm one for leaving them alone but there's always going to be a couple where I wish I had more time to get them exactly how I wanted, like Homer's heart attack in 'Homer's Triple Bypass'. A lot of people say how much they enjoy that scene but I look at it and think that I probably could have pushed myself a little bit further with it. Other ones that I worry about are only small details but I wish I could've fixed them at the time, in particular the famous scene in 'Deep Space Homer' where Homer is eating chips in space. There's a shot where he floats out of frame and it pans back down to Buzz and Race. They were supposed to glance at each other with a sort of 'what the?' look, but they didn't do

the eye lines right and the characters just continued to blink and look at Homer off-screen, so it was disappointing not to get that moment. Obviously, that's something only I would know . . . Well, until now.

Compare your feelings before the airing of 'Simpsons Roasting on an Open Fire' with the premiere of **The Simpsons Movie.**
I think I was more nervous for 'Simpsons Roasting on an Open Fire'. That felt like a bigger deal because we were starting a new thing. By the time of *The Simpsons Movie* premiere I was more confident in our work. I didn't know how people would respond but I knew we'd delivered what I'd intended. I'd already been to premieres of films I'd helped direct, whereas in 1989 I'd never directed a half hour of television before.

Is it true you once, after a few drinks, jokingly pitched the idea to James L. Brooks for the shorts to become a series at **The Tracey Ullman Show** *party?*
Apparently so! I don't remember it all too much, but I think it was just a case of me seeing Jim and thinking wow I really should introduce myself. When we were working on *The Tracey Ullman Show* it was always great knowing we were working on a project with James L. Brooks, one of the creators of comedy. I just hoped that one day I'd get to meet him so I could tell him I thought he'd done such a great job with everything. So when I saw him at the party I remember thanking him for everything he'd done in regards to adult animation on prime-time television, maybe I said all those other things about giving him the idea for the show too but I

really don't remember. I must have, though, because even Jim has since told me I did. The first time he addressed that conversation was at the 100th episode launch. Jim and I were just standing at the bar and he turned around and said something like 'David, do you remember the first time we met at that *Tracey Ullman Show* party? I remember it distinctly because it was the first time I'd met a Simpsons animator and you had such passion about it. It made me think, wow if this is what our animators are like then maybe we could make a series out of this.'

So, we have you to thank for The Simpsons?
I guess so! I suppose what it means is that if you ever meet anyone you admire you should just tell them how you really feel. I didn't create the show but that conversation certainly energised Jim's desire to follow through with his vision for *The Simpsons*.

Season 2 (1990-91)
In Conversation

DANDO: While the first season was intended to introduce us to the show's central characters, this season focused on giving them some substance. It's clear that the writers now had a better idea of the direction they wanted to take each character and what role they would play within the dynamic of the show.

MITCH: Season 2 was where my love for the show really took hold. I had some VHS tapes when I was younger, and before a time of constant reruns they were my only way to watch episodes, so for maybe three to four years episodes like the original 'Treehouse of Horror' or 'Two Cars in Every Garage and Three Eyes on Every Fish' were burned into my memory. I can only imagine how bizarre it must have been to see a prepubescent boy quoting Edgar Allan Poe's 'The Raven', or discussing the fickle nature of political campaigns, but I think most adults would have been less impressed if they knew the true source of my knowledge.

D: I've always loved David Silverman's direction in 'The Raven' segment. It's some of the most creative work ever done on the show. On the subject 'Treehouse of Horror', I think that's one of the big reasons that everything suddenly feels more familiar from a fan's perspective. That first inclusion kicked off an annual tradition that has spawned some of my favourite moments of all time. Plus, many of our favourite sub-characters like Comic Book Guy, Hans Moleman, Professor Frink and Troy McClure were being introduced at a rapid rate.

M: Definitely. There's none of that jarring sensation that Season 1 can give you when you go back and watch any of the Season 2 episodes.

D: Of all those who debuted this season, Lionel Hutz as Bart's shady lawyer in his case against Mr. Burns is by far the standout for me.

M: Outside of Hank Scorpio, I don't think there's been a better character introduction than Hutz. The day a man gives me a business card that turns into a sponge, I'll consider all technology to have advanced as far as it can go.

D: This season saw the show win yet another Emmy Award with 'Homer vs. Lisa and the 8th Commandment', which was actually written by freelance writer, Steve Pepoon. It's amazing to think that there was a time when fans like you and I could write a spec script for the show, with a chance of it becoming an actual episode.

M: I went as far as sending a spec-script over to Al Jean a little while ago, who was nice enough to respond personally, but he explained that there's a policy in place now where they can't read scripts that are sent in externally. I assume it's a blanket ban to prevent any possible charges of plagiarism. My suggestion that he hire me for two hours to read the script and then fire me fell on deaf ears.

D: Well, it was worth a try.

M: One thing that I see as a big shift in Season 2 is that the Simpsons themselves are more likeable. They are imperfect, for sure, but there's none of the malice towards each other that saw them electroshock each other in Season 1.

D: I think a large part of the credit for that has to go to James L. Brooks. He was often able to find the emotional key to an episode and his influence started to be felt more and more.

M: There are a few great examples of that, but the pick of them for me is 'Lisa's Substitute'. I love the two concurrent storylines in that episode, with Homer helping Bart run for Class President, and of course Lisa falling into a kind of love for Mr. Bergstrom.

D: I think everyone has had a Mr. Bergstrom enter their life at some point whether you realised it at the time or not. My Bergstrom was a teacher at primary school who would always teach us maths via songs to the tune of Beatles hits, such as 'Here Comes the Sun', which he called 'Here Comes the Sum'.

M: I'm willing to bet that 'Lucy In the Sky with Division' got more than one mention that year. The obvious answer to why this episode sticks out for so many people is the bittersweet goodbye at the train station, but as I understand, that's not your favourite moment from the episode.

D: No, for me the most powerful moment is when Homer is trying to comfort Lisa after their argument over the dinner table. He doesn't quite know what it is that he's done wrong, he just knows that he needs to fix it. 'Everyone special to me is under this roof' is one of the most brilliant lines we ever hear from Homer. This is the first time we see Lisa learn to accept her father for who he is, not what she wants him to be. While she may see Homer as an inconsiderate baboon, the loss of Bergstrom helps her to realise that Homer is the one man who won't ever leave her.

M: These moments of emotional truth are the defining common thread of the season as a whole. Be it Homer's relief at Bart not jumping Springfield Gorge, Grampa's heartache over the death of Bea . . .

D: Spoilers.

M: It was 26 years ago, I think we're in the clear. Anyway, Homer being belittled over his weight by Mr. Burns, even Smithers' distress about Burns possibly dying in 'Blood Feud'. Virtually every episode has a big emotional scene for the actors to sink their teeth into.

D: Some of my favourite guest stars are featured this season. Recurring guests such as Jon Lovitz and the late, great Phil Hartman joined the cast, legends of Hollywood and Broadway such as Dustin Hoffman (Mr. Bergstrom), Harvey Fierstein (Karl) and Danny DeVito (Herb Powell) were also beginning to jump on the *Simpsons* bandwagon.

M: What I really enjoyed about these guest stars is that none of them come across as stunt-casting, with each guest fitting in seamlessly to the *Simpsons* universe. I've always felt that Dustin Hoffman choosing to be credited as Sam Etic was an attempt to let the work speak for itself, and really, all the other actors disappear into their characters rather than just play up to being themselves. In later years, it started to feel like you weren't a star until you were on *The Simpsons*, almost like it was a bucket-list activity for celebrities, but here it feels more like a genuine effort to blend in and work with great material.

D: I guess the one exception to that is Ringo Starr as Marge's teen heart-throb. But even his performance is my favourite of the three Beatles to appear on the show.

M: He also does a great job of playing up to a larger version of himself, and acts quite well throughout.

D: It helps that his lines are eminently quotable. It was only recently when my wife's younger cousin painted us a picture at kindergarten, when he asked what I did with it I replied, 'I hung it on me fridge, you're quite an artist!'

M: If I had a dollar for every time I adopted a Liverpudlian accent and corrected French fries to be chips, I'd be half as wealthy as Ringo.

D: Getting back to Danny DeVito, usually when a show starts introducing 'long lost' family members it's a late-season act of desperation, but in the case of 'Brother, Where Art Thou?' the show succeeds in breaking the mould while staying true to itself.

M: Danny's performance as Herb is pitch perfect. He's one of the first people apart from Marge to love Homer unconditionally.

D: The irony being Herb Powell's love for his new-found half-brother blinds him to the destruction that Homer unknowingly caused to his automotive empire. A personal highlight is the phone call from Herb's team that results in him making them tell the family the opposite of everything that they just said. You can only imagine what their original description of Homer's hygiene must have been.

M: Of course, Season 2 also puts some huge focus on the development of already established characters. We get the first real non-family-focused story with Skinner falling in love with Patty, which was a big step for the writers.

D: You get the feeling that episode showed them they could really play with the wider universe, rather than just focus on the key players week to week.

M: And this season also gave a deeper understanding of Homer and Marge . . .

D: That came via the first flashback story with 'I Married Marge'. It's always fun to go back in time and visit the lives of the characters before we knew them, but this one served a key purpose: to provide an explanation as to how and why a woman like Marge ended up falling for Homer. As we see in the prom sequence, Homer may not have been the best looking, he may not have been the most intelligent, but if there was one thing he did excel in it was having an undeniable love for Marge. Artie Ziff was who Marge thought she wanted, Homer was who Marge knew she needed.

M: Homer and Marge's marriage is one of the greatest love stories ever told. They've been through hell and back but they've got an undying devotion to each other. The cornerstone of it all is Homer's love for Marge. Whenever somebody might ask what she sees in him, it's the fact that he loves her more than any man ever could, whereas Artie couldn't ever love anybody more than he loves himself. Homer might be ignorant of Marge at times, but when the chips are down, he'd give up everything for her. A love like that is special.

D: So, any final thoughts on Season 2?

M: It's a huge step forward to what will go on to become the best few years for the show, in my opinion, but it's still heading up the mountain to the peak. Essentially, if Season 1 is sea level and we are ascending Mount Everest, Season 2 is base camp one. We've got a long way to go, but we've learned a lot about what the future has in store.

'Bart Gets an F'
(Season 2, Episode 1)
Review by Dando

On the back of declining grades, Bart is faced with an ultimatum that if he doesn't pass his final test he will be forced to repeat the fourth grade (repeat the fourth grade, repeat the fourth grade). Desperate to pass, he turns to Martin, and then God, for assistance.

Much like 'Bart the Genius', I've always complimented 'Bart Gets an F' for being one of those episodes that many tend to forget came so early in the series. The story is as believable as it is relatable, positioning Bart as someone to sympathise with, rather than laugh at. Being the first episode to air following media scrutiny of the infamous 'Underachiever and Proud of It' merchandise, this feels like a direct response from the writers and show-runners, especially when Dr. Pryor makes a reference to the line during his meeting with Marge and Homer. James L. Brooks denied any retaliation claims, so perhaps it was just coincidental timing.

By Season 2, FOX knew that they had a bona fide hit on their hands and informed *The Simpsons* team that they'd now be moving to Thursday nights to compete with the #1 rated show at the time, *The Cosby Show.*

With this episode airing at the height of Bartmania, Brooks hand-picked it to be the first soldier in the Bill vs. Bart rivalry. Cosby may have won the first battle by 0.1 in the ratings, but to this day 'Bart Gets an F' remains the highest rated episode of *The Simpsons* in history.

We get to see an emotional side of Bart that the writers only tend to bring out when absolutely necessary, an ace in the hole that helps turn a good episode into a great one. It worked in 'Marge Be Not Proud', and it works just as well here with Bart's outpouring of tears upon failing yet another test. Nancy's performance of utter heartbreak matched with Silverman's genius direction of sinking Bart's face into his paper to seemingly hide from the inevitable, makes for one of my favourite Bart moments of all time.

It was important that Bart's laziness and lack of effort at school came with a consequence, and that said consequence was something he truly feared. During the first season Bart would often appear unfazed by punishments, passing the blame and not taking responsibility for his actions (i.e. spray-painting his 'I am a weiner' mural of Principal Skinner). This was different, as writer David M. Stern raised the stakes beyond a mere detention.

The idea of being left behind whilst all your friends move on to the next grade is terrifying for any child, and I'm sure it's a situation millions of so-called underachievers have actually lived through. It's a real-life scenario that would strike a nerve with any younger viewer. Although Bart's premonition may be a little exaggerated, the fact that he envisions himself remaining in the fourth grade until he's a middle-aged man with a peptic ulcer and a wife hawking him for a new car, certainly demonstrates that he understands the crisis he has created for himself.

With his behaviour at the beginning, such as faking an illness to avoid the test and copying answers from Milhouse, it's amazing that we can still feel sorry for this child who probably doesn't deserve our sincerity. For me, the key moment is Bart's reaction when Dr. Pryor issues the ultimatum that he may have to repeat. Exasperated, Bart snaps and refers to himself as 'dumb as a post'. Seeing this normally confident boy so down on himself makes me want to jump into the TV and reassure him that's he's smarter than he thinks.

The key to this story isn't Bart identifying his problem, it's how he addresses it. He truly wants to work hard and improve his grades, which is why after a not-so reassuring conversation with Otto, he concedes and asks for assistance from teacher's pet, and then nemesis, Martin Prince. It may not seem like a big deal, but in a world where social status in the schoolyard means everything, it's as desperate as it gets.

What's interesting here is the way Stern explores the impact of Bart's influence on the usual do-gooder Martin. The two boys seemingly reverse roles, as Bart unintentionally opens Martin's eyes to the world outside of the classroom. When he ditches Bart to go to the arcade because 'life's too short for tests', it once again leaves Bart with nowhere to turn and reinforces a sense of sympathy that eventually pays off in a big way during the episode's climax.

With his plan failed and his back against the wall, Bart resorts to 'the last refuge of a scoundrel' and prays to God for a miracle. Thankfully he gets not one, but two. The first being 'Snow Day', the funnest day in the history of Springfield. The other being his sister Lisa, who takes on the role of guardian angel as she guides her easily distracted brother on the correct path to studying, instead of having snowball fights with Burnsie. She may not get as much credit as the big guy upstairs, but Lisa is just as important to Bart's success as anybody.

At the core, 'Bart Gets an F' is a true underdog story. It silenced the critics (whether intentionally or not), adding an unexplored layer to the show's main protagonist at the time. It's possible to refer to Bart as an anti-hero, but for me he's just a kid who has yet to learn the responsibilities that come with his actions. This episode took the first steps towards teaching him that valuable lesson.

What did we learn?

The potential for mischief varies inversely with one's proximity to the authority figure.

'The War of the Simpsons'
(Season 2, Episode 20)
Review by Mitch

Homer's drunken behaviour at a party causes a rift in his marriage. He heads to a marriage retreat with Marge to try and repair the damage, and sneak in a spot of fishing. Back at home, Bart and Lisa take advantage of Grampa, but get in over their heads.

When Dando and I were discussing which episodes of Season 2 should be broken down, we had a really difficult time settling on which version of Homer we wanted to go with. There are many different shades of Homer, and Season 2 has them all on display. There's Homer the Incompetent, as seen in 'Oh Brother, Where Art Thou'; Homer the Lover, as seen in 'The Way We Was'; Homer the Sinner, as seen in 'Homer vs. Lisa and the Eighth Commandment'; Competitive and driven Homer, on display in 'Dead Putting Society'; Ignorant Homer, in 'One Fish, Two Fish, Blowfish, Bluefish'. Finally, there's dancing Homer, as seen in 'Dancin' Homer'. We argued back and forth over the merits of each, trying to figure out which is the true version of the character, until we realised that 'The War of the Simpsons' is one of the very few episodes to encapsulate all sides of Homer's personality. It takes some risks by doing so, particularly as it's the more negative aspects of Homer on display early. I remember as a young child watching this and struggling to figure out why anybody would like this guy at all. He's the worst kind of drunk. He's loud, obnoxious, objectifies women and offends everybody in the room. In another age, he may well run for President, but in 1991 it was quite a shock to see something like this on TV.

As an adult, I look back and see that what made Homer so successful is that he's one of the most relatable men on the small screen. That's not to say we all share all his traits, but in a broad sense, most of us share some of them. This connection is enhanced here by the central premise being a realistic one, yet one that again is not often seen on television. The opening scenes of Marge and Homer making last-minute preparations for a dinner party (a bygone ritual where we would invite friends over to judge us and our possessions) could well have been transcripts from any number of houses in the 90s. As Homer descends into drunken boorishness, and his guests struggle more and more to hide their contempt, the party starts to describe the worst parts of his marriage.

While the party shows Homer at his worst, it's also the episode at its funniest. It's part of what keeps us from turning on Homer completely. From his opening mispronunciation of hors d'oeuvres (Horse Doovers) through to maniacally screaming at a man he's never met and threatening to quit working for him, Homer is mostly harmless. It's only when he leers at Maude Flanders that he truly crosses the line. The party also enables us to see citizens of Springfield mingling in a way we haven't before. Flanders shows his ability to make more than just Homer jealous, as he jokes to Moe about his degree in mixology ('Pfft . . . College Boy'). Ever the rule-breaker, Bart sneaks his way down to the party despite his supposed bedtime. Including him here was a nice touch, taking me back to a time when the increasingly loud voices of an adult party would prove too intriguing to ignore.

The way Homer is woken the next morning is telling. Anybody who has ever had their significant other wake them by vacuuming *into* their head knows that they've got some serious 'splainin to do. Homer's desperate attempt to remember what had happened the night before leads to one of my favourites of his distortions of reality, as he pictures himself sitting at the Algonquin Round Table, quipping of wet suits, dry martinis and fake flies in ice cubes. It's a classic example of the drunk we wish we were vs. the drunk we really are.

Homer and Marge heading off to the marriage retreat opens the door for the B plot: Grampa babysitting Bart and Lisa. This almost plays out like a short film within the larger confines of everything else that is going on. It has all the makings of a great short: a clear concept that's well established, an escalation of events, and an unexpected ending. Bart and Lisa taking advantage of Grampa is wish fulfilment for grandchildren everywhere, but Grampa's revenge show's that there are few tricks that older people aren't aware of. Grampa getting the upper hand doesn't happen often, so it's great to see him genuinely outwit the kids.

Like so many of the early episodes, the sensibilities of

James L. Brooks are felt in the final scenes of Homer and Marge's camp. There's a line in *Good Will Hunting* that real loss is only something that happens when you love somebody more than you love yourself. As Homer rows back to shore after having caught the mythical General Sherman, this is exactly what he is confronted with. It's here that his love shines through. In a heartbeat, he tosses the fish back to the waters below. It's the moment that you realise Homer would give up anything for Marge. He may not be a perfect man, but he will love her more than any other man ever could. What began with a relatable moment between husband and wife ends with another. It's not a perfect marriage, but few are. That's what's so perfect about it.

What did we learn?

You can't avenge your partner's death with a pea-shooter.

Season 3 (1991-92)
In Conversation

DANDO: Season 3 contained the series' first 'classic' episodes in 'Stark Raving Dad' and 'Homer at the Bat'. That's not to say that those that came before aren't great in their own right, but these both took *The Simpsons* to the next level. Even people who aren't avid Simpsons viewers know of them, in fact the latter recently earned Homer Simpson a place in the Baseball Hall of Fame.

MITCH: That, right there, says a lot about the power and shared love of *The Simpsons*.

D: This was the first episode to win in the ratings war with *The Cosby Show*. However, it didn't go over well with some of the cast members. Harry Shearer believed it focused too much on the guests and not the main cast, which is a fair point, but as a fan watching from the outside it's impossible not to enjoy the hilarious exploits of the power plant softball team. Regardless of the nine MLB players, Homer's slow-mo reaction to his home run, Charlie using his sister's wooden leg as a bat or even Mr. Burns being knocked off-screen by a softball in the batting cages are just some of the moments that make this a favourite amongst so many.

M: What amazes me about this episode is the quality of performance derived from so many non-actors. It helps that they all seem to have a true understanding of the comedy of the show. Be it Wade Boggs getting into a bar fight with Barney, Steve Sax's cries for help falling on deaf ears with the police, or Mike Scioscia getting down and dirty in a blue-collar job, all athletes are happy to play up to this crazy version of themselves.

D: Let's not forget Mattingly's sideburns.

M: My favourite thing about that is that he still *tries* to please this crazy manager. Anyway, I think this show-cases something almost uniquely American about sports stars – there are so many larger than life characters that they slot perfectly into film and TV a lot of the time. Think of Keith Hernandez in *Seinfeld*, LeBron James in *Trainwreck*, Or Shaq in . . . well . . . maybe not Shaq.

D: In comparison to 'Homer at the Bat', 'Stark Raving Dad' featured only one guest star, however that's all it needed. Known to many as 'the one with Michael Jackson', this episode is one of those few times where the guest is bigger than the show.

M: It's funny how often I forget that title relates to this episode. MJ casts such a huge shadow that you almost forget about the plot of Homer being thought to be insane on the grounds of wearing a pink shirt to work. Obviously, this episode predates the concept of the metrosexual male.

D: Jackson's performance was handled so uniquely that it almost feels like an in-joke between Jackson and those working behind the scenes.

M: It's almost like life imitating art imitating life. It was confusing enough that Dustin Hoffman credit himself as Sam Etic, but Michael Jackson starring as a guy who only *pretends* to be Michael Jackson is a stroke of baffling genius.

D: It was a swindle that fooled naïve young Dando into thinking it wasn't actually Jackson, that it was some impostor named John Jay Smith all along. The truth is even more complicated, as Michael recorded the dialogue while an impersonator named Kipp Lennon, who was hand-picked by Michael, sang the songs. However, Michael did write 'Happy Birthday Lisa' himself.

M: Ensuring millions of girls named Lisa around the world had a song that would be played by friends every year from that point on.

D: The King of Pop may no longer be with us, but that little gem of a tune is a gift that will last a lifetime.

M: Aside from tentpole moments featuring massive guest stars. Season 3 really brings a focus on relationships. At the core of 'Lisa's Pony' and 'Lisa the Greek' is her relationship with Homer. 'When Flanders Failed' is largely about the conflict between Ned and Homer. Even an episode like 'Dog of Death' is a perfect exploration of the love we can feel for our canine friends. Of course, in true *Simpsons* style, the characters are rarely well equipped to handle these emotions.

D: It was interesting to see the writers incorporate Bart into actual love-based stories this season. In 'Bart the Lover' he toys with Mrs. Krabappel's emotions as he plays the role of her love interest Woodrow.

M: There's a bit of a recurring theme with Bart where he starts a prank without realising the ways it can get out of hand, and then feels remorseful for it afterwards. 'Radio Bart' being another example of that.

D: The way he finds enjoyment out of making Mrs. K think she's found 'the one' is downright cruel, but the way he responds to the situation once he sees Edna's reaction after being stood up at the restaurant shows a maturity well beyond his years.

M: Yeah, it shows that there's no real malice at play, just a lack of understanding.

D: He later becomes jealous when Milhouse starts dating Samantha Stankey in 'Bart's Friend Falls in Love'. Again, as he does his best to break up their relationship, Bart comes across rather poorly. In saying that, you can slightly forgive him since you can't expect a 10-year-old boy to understand what love is.

M: If only he'd listened to more Haddaway.

D: In a sign of the show's expansion, we see more and more of the show's sub-characters receiving entire episodes dedicated to giving them more depth; we learn of Krusty's tragic past in 'Like Father, Like Clown', Flanders steals our hearts in 'When Flanders Failed' and Moe's selfishness simply shines in 'Flaming Moes'.

M: There's also a bit of a forgotten gem of Sideshow Bob's schemes in 'Black Widower'. Given her frequent lack of empathy, it makes sense that Selma would fall for Springfield's most notorious villain. Crucially, this is the first time we see how evil Bob can be, as it's his first murder plot. He is also yet again foiled and sent back to prison by Bart, setting up for further acts of revenge in the future. It's forever changed the way I hear 'MacGyver' in my head.

D: Those examples were all successful in giving the characters some substance; however when it came to 'The Otto Show', it didn't quite hit the mark. It started strong with the hilarious Spinal Tap concert, which I'm sure Shearer and the boys had an absolute blast performing.

M: That troupe always slip so perfectly back into those characters. I'm sure that fans of *This is Spinal Tap* would rate this as one of their favourite episodes based on the first 10 minutes alone. From a half-inflated Satan, to promises of no encore, to the assertion that they have great sales in the 'other garia', this is classic *Tap*. It made me wonder if it was scripted or if the writers just had big blocks of '[Insert improv here]' for their scenes.

D: By the end of the episode, however, I think I actually *disliked* Otto. Some characters are best left to the one-liners and Otto is a perfect example. He doesn't have a voice that you want to hear speak large chunks of dialogue, so when you combine that with a story that bases its jokes on how pathetic he is, you're left with somewhat of a failed experiment.

M: What the second half struggles to do is find any sub-stance in Otto, at a time when the comedy in the show almost entirely derived from character. He doesn't really evolve, he doesn't learn anything, and Harry Shearer is only really given one note to play him with. The second half still has some great lines, and an inspired *Happy Days* parody where Otto lives with the family, but it just lacks that meaty hook of so many of the episodes that came before it.

D: However, it's not all doom and gloom. Skinner's slow descent into madness while trying to merge into oncoming traffic as the school's replacement bus driver is easily one of my favourite moments of the season.

M: I guess there's only one real way to summarise the episode . . .

D: Good show?

M: Yeah, quite good.

D: The season ends on a high, bringing back Herb Powell for 'Brother, Can You Spare Two Dimes?'.

M: This wasn't originally part of the season's run, airing in August where the season finished in May, but when watched as part of the DVD box sets it's an undeniably strong point to go out on.

D: Sadly, 25 years on, we're still no closer to a baby translator.

M: For me, Season 3 is one step closer to the show hitting its absolute peak. It shows glimpses of what can be done, but there are still one or two missteps along the way.

D: The strike rate is a lot higher, though.

M: For sure. We also got introduced to Fat Tony for the first, and possibly the best, time in 'Bart the Murderer'. I spent years rather pretentiously ordering a Manhattan in bars all over Melbourne purely to make a *Simpsons* reference. I hated the taste, but I just couldn't help myself.

'Like Father, Like Clown'
(Season 3, Episode 6)
Review by Mitch

When Krusty comes to visit the Simpsons for dinner, it is revealed that he hasn't seen his father for 25 years. Bart and Lisa attempt to reunite Krusty with his dad, a rabbi who never accepted the fact that Krusty had become a clown.

Growing up as I did in a non-religious household in a small town south of Melbourne, I had very little exposure to different faiths as a child. I was largely aware of Christianity, but the Jewish faith was not something I really came across in my day to day life. Given that, it's remarkable that 'Like Father, Like Clown' has had such a long-lasting impact on me. It speaks of the clever way that universal themes of love and family are interwoven with several meticulously researched references to religious text and culture.

For the second and final time, Brad Bird has a directing credit, assisting first-timer Jeffrey Lynch. Brad is arguably one of the best animation directors in the world, his credits including Pixar's *Ratatouille*, *The Incredibles*, and my favourite animated film of all time, *The Iron Giant*. It's a real shame that he only directed two *Simpsons* episodes in his tenure, as the direction here is stellar. Despite the 22-minute run-time, this *feels* like a feature production. The use of shade and lighting on the characters' faces in particular gives the appearance of a work of art. A still shot of the family waiting on Krusty, drenched in twilight, is a beautiful example of a shot you can really drink in. There are little moments of camerawork that add to the feeling of the direction being on a higher plane. See Miss Penny-candy turn her back on a photo of Krusty as the camera pans away as she emphasises 'Miss'. The New-York-inspired flashback to Lower East Springfield is so faithful that you can almost smell the matzah ball soup. Finally, the interior of the Jewish Deli feels so realistic I half expected to see Billy Crystal walk in and order a sandwich. Being so early in Season 3 when animation could still be patchy, it really makes this episode stand out as being different.

The entrenchment in Jewish faith to an outsider could have been a roadblock in being able to really connect to the story. To skirt around that, the issue at hand is wisely kept very relatable. At its core, this is a story of a boy trying to find his father's approval. The flashbacks to Rabbi Krustofski (played by Jackie Mason) are some of my favourites to watch as an adult. The rabbi breaking into the bathroom to find a young Krusty squirting himself with a seltzer bottle is a great example of an X-rated joke told in a PG format, and one of those golden moments of *The Simpsons* simultaneously operating on two different levels. It's funny as a kid because Krusty got squirted in the face. It's funny as an adult because . . . well . . . you know.

Given that this virtually served as my introduction to the Jewish faith, it's a nice touch that the episode only displays positive stereotypes of religion. The Rabbi is always deep in thought, always seeking more knowledge, and is a respected member of the community. Even Christianity, usually the butt of religious jokes on the show, is treated with a softer touch. The only laughs at the expense of religion come from the overwhelming positivity of the religious community. When religious leaders are asked if they ever doubt God's existence on talk show *Gabbin' about God*, the three emphatic 'no's' are the only time they all agree on something.

Given the fractured nature of the Krustofski family, it's fitting that the close bond between Bart and Lisa is the catalyst for reconciliation. I've always loved the episodes where Bart and Lisa team up to solve something that adults can't. The combination of Lisa's intimidating intelligence and Bart's tenacity and inability to see when he is being a genuine nuisance forms a dynamic that can get around any obstacle. Their action is well contrasted with Krusty's lack of it. With each passing day, he appears more sluggish and depressed on his show, but the scenes themselves don't suffer from the same malaise. Perhaps it is owed to the stereotype of the sad clown, perhaps it's the direction, or perhaps it's Dan's acting, but whatever the cause, there's something perversely hilarious about watching Krusty break down live on television. The fact that it's an incredibly violent *Itchy & Scratchy* cartoon that sends him over the edge probably helps. Through the maiming and the bloodshed, his focus is on the deeper theme of Itchy having a good time with his dad.

If nothing else, 'Like Father, Like Clown' showcases the talents of Brad Bird and is interesting to reflect upon from a historical perspective, to see the early work of the animation maestro. In a more immediate sense, it lacks one-liners but has enough absurdity to keep you laughing throughout the episode. There is an adage to never meet your heroes as they can only let you down. Fortunately, watching Bart meet his hero has the opposite effect for us in the most polished example of *The Simpsons* to date.

What did we learn?

Mel Brooks is Jewish.

'Colonel Homer'
(Season 3, Episode 20)
Review by Dando

After feeling Marge has robbed him of his dignity, Homer goes for a drive to be alone for a while. Stopping at a redneck bar, he discovers Lurleen Lumpkin, waitress and songstress extraordinaire. Determined to make her voice known to more people, he becomes her manager and helps her cut her first album. Marge starts to fear for her marriage as Homer spends increasing amounts of time with Lurleen, and it becomes clear that she sees him as more than her manager.

'Colonel Homer' is an episode that took me over two decades to appreciate. With my family being such huge fans of country music, I was forced to endure countless hours as a child listening to tales of heartbreak and sorrow from the likes of Slim Whitman and Conway Twitty, resulting in a real disdain for the genre. So, as you can imagine, the thought of a *Simpsons* episode based around a country and western singer was anything but appealing to me. It wasn't until we recently went back to review the episode for our podcast that I discovered just how magical it truly was.

Just prior to our review it became apparent that I

could barely remember anything about 'Colonel Homer', besides the fact that it had Lurleen Lumpkin and Homer wore a white suit, which was probably due to the fact that I hadn't watched it in over 15 years. It was rather exciting having the opportunity to go back and watch an episode from the show's golden era for essentially the first time, yet once I did, it left me disappointed to realise what I'd missed out on all these years.In his first and only solo writing credit, Matt Groening produced a beautiful tale of lust and jealousy. If this was the kind of material Groening was capable of, it's a shame he didn't put pen to paper more often. By choosing to focus on raw emotion rather than humour, the story has a more realistic feel to it than the others based around Marge and Homer's marriage. Julie Kavner's acting in the scene where Marge asks Homer if he is having an affair is about as powerful as the character gets. You can hear not only her anger, but the fear that she may be losing the love of her life. You forget that you are watching a cartoon as poor Marge is left alone and helpless to dwell on what the future may hold for her family.

Another gut-wrenching moment is when Marge almost concedes defeat as she realises Homer is more interested in his suit than to listening about Maggie cutting her first tooth. It's almost 'too real', if that's even possible, which is probably why Groening felt the need to end the scene with a bit of humour as Bart says, 'as much as I hate that man right now, you've gotta love that suit'.

At times, particularly in the moments just mentioned, Homer can come across as an inconsiderate jerk, the only saving grace being that he is completely oblivious to Lurleen's advances. That said, he still makes the deliberate and conscious decision to ignore Marge's plea for reassurance as he puts his wants and needs ahead of hers, even going so far as to spend their life savings on Lurleen's record without consulting Marge first. Put yourself in her shoes and you can truly understand the angst she feels towards this woman who is seemingly stealing her husband from under her nose.

Speaking of Lurleen, Beverly D'Angelo was an incredible choice for the role, as she brings a wholesome yet flirtatious flavour to the character that most men couldn't resist. Groening apparently met D'Angelo at a party at Frank Zappa's house and called her in to audition after her standout performance as Patsy Cline in *Coal Miner's Daughter*. Not only did she sing the songs in the episode, she also wrote both 'Your Wife Don't Understand You' and 'I Bagged a Homer'. The charm of her performance is that although Lurleen is openly willing to become a homewrecker, you still don't hate her for it. She's a beautiful, talented woman desperate for true love; it's just unfortunate that she found it ten years too late. It would be very easy for us as viewers to despise her for her actions, especially after meeting Marge and the kids at the recording studio, yet somehow D'Angelo manages to leave you feeling sorry for this poor woman who, despite now having the world as her oyster, will never get what she truly wants.

Once Homer had become aware of Lurleen's feelings for him, it was important for Groening not to let him linger on too long, deciding which path he wanted to choose. In saying that, it's understandable how confused he was, since up until this point Marge had been the only woman to ever show interest in Homer sexually. As

Homer's romantic life flashes before his eyes, the move from rejection after rejection to Marge's promise to love him for the rest of her life is beautiful and powerful enough to reduce a married man to tears. When I think about that scene now, I picture my own wife in place of Marge, and it gives me chills every time that I do. Without a doubt, the episode's closing sequence is my absolute favourite Homer and Marge moment of all time. The look of despair on Marge's face as she lies naked in an empty bed, thinking she's about to watch the last remnants of her marriage disappear, only to learn that the man of her dreams is still by her side is, as I mentioned at the beginning, magical. No words are needed while Lurleen sings 'Stand by Your Manager'; the animation is perfection as the two simply look into each other's eyes and realise that nobody will ever come between them.

Besides delivering more goosebumps than this fool could handle, 'Colonel Homer' helped me realise that I actually no longer hate country music: if anything, it now reminds me of being home and surrounded by my loved ones. As this episode shows us, music is a powerful tool. It was the driving force behind Homer's motives and the only way Lurleen could communicate her feelings for him. It's amazing that an episode I once avoided as a child, due to its soundtrack, has now become one of my favourites because of it.

What did we learn?

Everyone should own at least one white suit.

Talking to Gods

It's October 2015, and we are on the outskirts of Melbourne riding a tram filled with cosplayers; some of the characters we recognise, many of them we don't. As our eyes dart around the carriage looking at these people brave enough to bare their soul through the costumes they wear, we ironically become filled with a painfully real sense of naked vulnerability. At every stop the crowd grows thicker with Batmen and Harley Quinns. As the numbers count up, we start to count down. We are getting closer to AMC Expo, where we are scheduled to interview Maggie Roswell. Would she look at us and see two emperors? Or two impostors without clothing?

Three months earlier, this was a situation we only allowed ourselves occasional moments to fantasise about. We were always very aware of the fact that Geelong was a long way away from the studios of LA, but getting the opportunity to speak to a cast member was a goal from the start. In fact, in the very first episode of Four Finger Discount we anticipated what it would be like to interview Harry Shearer. Back then it was just a pipe dream . . . surely it could never really happen.

It's with no small degree of gratitude that we say we owe every bit of our show's success to Nikki Isordia. Nikki was the first person to agree to be interviewed for our podcast. In doing so, she gave us a sense of validation that we could never have felt on our own. To think that somebody who works on *that* show was aware of *our* show?! It made us believe that we belonged. That we had credibility. That we were, in a small sense of the word, emperors.

From those beginnings, we have been fortunate enough to secure exclusive interviews with the likes of Joe Mantegna, the aforementioned Maggie Roswell, storyboard director and fellow Australian Matthew Schofield, and the incomparable Harry Shearer. What we were struck by in each of these interviews is the incredible generosity and sincerity they all displayed. As soon as we met Maggie, we realised we needn't have worried about feeling unworthy. Like so many of the every-woman characters she plays, she put us at ease with her effusive welcome. It felt more like popping around to visit an aunty for a coffee than it felt like an interview. The sight of her breaking into an impromptu rendition of 'Cut Every Corner' as we recorded guerrilla style in the cafeteria is one of our life's great memories.

Indeed, this was our experience with each interview. Matt Schofield put up with a bad internet connection and dying batteries to spend two hours with us on a Sunday afternoon discussing the show from an animator's perspective. Joe Mantegna was kind enough to wait until after a delay caused by a daylight savings mishap, and still spoke to us for longer than we first thought we would get. For Harry, it was our turn to wait, pacing back and forth as he completed other media commitments. Between radio networks and TV shows, he may have done 15 interviews before speaking to us, but you wouldn't have known it for a second. Here's a guy who has done it all, but he couldn't have been warmer. No matter what happens to us in life, we can say that we made *the* Harry Shearer laugh once. These are gifts that can never be taken away.

We wanted to include excerpts of these interviews for those who have bought this book but haven't listened to the show, for two reasons. One: they give a fascinating insight into what goes into making the show, or a character, come to life. Two: to include this tribute as a thank-you to everybody who made it possible. When we look back on that day in our lives on a tram in Melbourne surrounded by elaborate costumes, we don't see ourselves in emperors' clothing. Rather, we see ourselves dressed as Wayne and Garth, kneeling at the temple of the Simpsons' gods as we exclaim, 'We're not worthy.'

Maggie Roswell

Maggie started working for The Simpsons *in 1989, but didn't become a series regular until the second season with the introduction of Helen Lovejoy. Known for her ability to voice 'every-woman' characters, her other notable characters include Luann Van Houten, Miss Hoover, Maude Flanders and Shary Bobbins.*

On whether the job was ever taken for granted due to its success:
For me, no. Nobody really knew how it was going to go. And even though it's gone [on to great success] I quit the tenth year and came back in the thirteenth, because I went to Colorado, and then they killed Maude Flanders and there was a whole . . . thing.

On recording remotely from Colorado rather than a round-table:

We were kind of trailblazers initially – originally it was not the best deal [for FOX]. Now, Hank Azaria is in New York doing a TV show. Julie Kavner can be away sometimes. We don't sit around the table as much any more. Because the characters are so well known and we have such great interaction, and we'd done that for so many years, there still is that warmth among the characters. But that's only because those first ten years we were around the table doing it together for eight hours at a time.

On her favourite moments from those early table-reads:

Watching Harry really realise how much Smithers was in love with Mr. Burns, to watch his face as he was delivering it . . . The table-read is really a blast. Harry would rip open [the script] and he wouldn't have read it before, but he'd go through it and be brilliant. Other people would have gone through and marked their lines. But that is *really* fun. I remember doing one with Mel Gibson . . . I was so thrilled that it was MEL GIBSON. I was looking down, and then I looked up a little, and then quickly looked back down. At one point I looked up and he was looking at me, and I went 'tee-hee', and I thought, 'Oh my God . . . did I really just do that?'

On discovering a voice:

Well, Maude Flanders had to be married to Ned. So, discovering the type of person that he would get [married to] – someone who was really nice, because that's the kind of guy he is. Then you had Helen Lovejoy,

Reverend Lovejoy's wife who was just everyone you've ever met that you go 'Oh, I just hate her!' But she'll smile at your face and then stab you in the back. Miss Hoover was actually born from the episode 'Brush with Greatness': [when] the painting of Burns is unveiled a woman steps out of the crowd and says, 'He's bad, but he'll die.' They liked that voice and thought it would be perfect for Miss Hoover.

On being a fan:
I love the show! It's wild for us, too, because when you're reading the script you'll see all the little things that they're doing, but you don't see it come to life . . . it takes a year for us to do the show . . . so by the time you see it you hardly even remember it.

Stepping into the shoes of Shary Bobbins:
That's the only vocal impression I do. They thought Julie Andrews was going to do the show. They were going back and forth because at that point they were thinking they would do an *actual* Mary Poppins. Eventually they figured, OK, it's not going to happen, so I got to do it. To be able to 'do' her was so brilliant!

Matt Schofield

Australian-born Matt Schofield has worked in the animation department since 1999, and has directed several episodes. Prior to his time on the show, Matt worked on the critically acclaimed animated films The Iron Giant *and* Prince of Egypt.

The intimidation factor of working on such a big-time show:

My first time doing character layout was on 'Take my Wife, Sleaze' where Homer starts a bikie gang. At the end of the episode, there is a rival bikie leader voiced by John Goodman. He and Homer have a kind of sword-fight, but using motorbikes, and I had to draw *that* as my way of being dropped into the deep end. So that was sort of intimidating, but you're always being asked to draw something different, so it really pushes you in terms of your skill level.

How direction/storyboarding can differ, and how it can enhance a show:

When you're directing, you've got three months to kind of shepherd an episode through from start to finish ... whereas now that I'm just doing the storyboard I've got two weeks and then I've gotta get onto the next show. Clarity is something that we are always striving for: to make the jokes read as clearly as possible, whether that's through the action itself, or whether it's through the way that a shot is composed so that everything is able to be clearly seen.

Favourite piece of animation:

The thing that comes to mind immediately is something that I saw before I'd even started working on the show. It was from the episode where Homer goes to clown college, and he's riding this really tiny bicycle. I remember seeing that piece of footage and thinking that it was so well done, it struck me that the animation on this show was great. Animation at that time had a reputation for being cheaply done. For me, that was quite eye-opening.

On the Simpsons *animation style:*
Matt Groening always has said that he wants the show to feel like a real-life situation that just happens to be animated. That's also gone into things in terms of the animation style where we don't do a lot of 'cartoony' animation. There's no stretch-and-squash, they don't distort their faces. They might go into it sometimes for a joke, but it's not like a Warner Bros. cartoon, or a Tex Avery cartoon where the characters' eyes will literally pop out of their heads. All of that reinforces the feeling that they *are* real characters.

His favourite characters to draw:
I really like Moe, because he's so reprehensible. He's always Mr. Sadsack. You can do really fun expressions on him because he's got really big, kind of 'caveman' brows. Mr. Burns is kind of fun to draw when you draw him wide-eyed, and draw him a bit cute. I think it's fun to draw him like that because he is so evil, it's something a bit out of the ordinary.

Joe Mantegna

Famous to Simpsons *fans for his role as Fat Tony, Joe Mantegna has over 200 film and TV credits, including* Godfather: Part III, *and more recently* Criminal Minds.

Not confined to the screen, Joe won the Best Actor Tony Award for his role as Ricky Roma in Glengarry Glen Ross.

On landing the role of Fat Tony:

They offered me that role right when *Godfather III* came out, probably because they knew that since I was playing the heavy in the film, I'd be a natural to play Fat Tony. I was just thrilled. I thought it was only going to be one episode and that would be that. Little did I know that the character would resonate and I would wind up doing as many episodes as I've done, and still continue to do.

On 'finding' the character:

They don't really give you much direction, but what they do give you are the words. As an actor, it's your job to find the character within that dialogue. I had an image [in my mind] with the name *Fat* Tony, so right away I knew the guy was going to be fat, so I knew I could sell that. Since it was the first time he was appearing, I didn't know what he was going to look like. There was no prototype design because I think they drew the character to the voice, since we record the dialogue way ahead of the animation.

On the inspiration behind the voice:

Godfather III had just come out, so I didn't want it to sound like Joey Zasa. I didn't want to use my own voice, I wanted Fat Tony to be somebody else. I basically tapped into the voice of one of my dearest uncles, Willie, who just passed away a couple of years ago. He was no gangster, he just knew a lot of those types of characters.

He'd quit smoking 20 years prior, but had developed cancer in his throat so they removed one of his vocal cords, meaning he then sounded like [Fat Tony].

One time I brought Uncle Willie to a recording session and I said to the writers 'I want you to meet the real Fat Tony'. Of course he introduced himself and they all laughed, saying 'Oh my God! Now we know who we can use if Joe's not here!'

On what input he has into the character:
At times I've come up with ad-libs. Sometimes they use them and sometimes they don't, especially on the episodes that are very Fat Tony heavy. I remember once we put in an ad-lib that had something to do with Bob Hope, but between the recording and the time it aired, Bob Hope had died, so they switched it back to the original line. Sometimes they've indicated that they wanted Fat Tony to speak some Italian phrases but didn't know what words to use, so I would provide them with Italian slang that would resonate with people who understood it.

Comparing the recording studio between then and now:
They had this little makeshift recording studio in the basement of the FOX lot, and I remember they just had this microphone setup in a circle in this room with a ping-pong table. I mean that was it, it was very low profile, no frills, they didn't know how long they were gonna be there so they just stuck up a recorder and that's that. Well now you go to FOX and they have their own building. There's the Marge Simpson sound stage, they even have their own murals painted on walls.

On the vibe of the read-throughs:
That's actually more exciting than the recording, because what you do is you go into this big room and everyone sits around this big table. All the actors are there and then they invite guests to sit around the room. It's an exciting hour because you get to meet everybody and see the actors actually read the characters. It's become one of the hottest tickets in town.

On his passion for The Simpsons:
I'm probably still making the same money I was when I did my first [appearance], but for me this is not what I do for a living. *The Simpsons* is just this fun thing I do. They know when they write Fat Tony that I want to play the character, I don't want them to get someone else who sounds like me. As long as they keep writing the character I'm glad to do it because I only do one or two each season anyway. I'm flattered that the character has taken on such importance to *The Simpsons*, so like I said, to me it's just about doing a character and I've never looked at it as a job. When I think of *The Simpsons* it brings a smile to my face.

Harry Shearer

Beginning his career as a child actor alongside Abbot and Costello, there's virtually nothing that Harry Shearer hasn't done in entertainment. Best known for his role in Spinal Tap *prior to* The Simpsons, *his voice credits include Mr. Burns, Smithers, Reverend Lovejoy,*

Kent Brockman, Dr. Hibbert, Otto, Rainier Wolfcastle, Ned Flanders and many more. He has written three books and these days can occasionally be found performing alongside his singer/songwriter wife, Judith Owen.

On when he realised The Simpsons *was a success:*
Somewhere in the middle of the first season it seemed apparent. FOX was a fledgling station yet we were having this rapid spike of popularity. Then because of our popularity, the network got more and more popular, to the point where I think three or four years into our run, Rupert Murdoch made a huge money bid for American football and got it away from CBS. When he did that, a lot of the former CBS stations switched to FOX because they wanted to keep football. So suddenly we found ourselves from being on Channel 54 now being on Channel 2, which was much more accessible on people's TV dials in those days. By that point we knew we were set in for quite a run.

On whether he's ever forgotten how to do a voice:
Not really. The only thing that ever really happened in that way, was we started recording Season 2 before Season 1 had gone to air, and I'd remembered most of the [voices], but I'd slipped a little in my memory of how Burns sounded, so he sounded a little different from Season 2 onward. I think Dan Castellaneta had the same issue with Homer. In Season 1 he was more knowingly doing an homage to an older American comedy performer, Eddie Mayehoff.

On the show's history with Christian conservative groups:
I have to say, I realised how long we'd been on the air around Season 15, because at the beginning when the show rocketed to popularity, the first wave of publicity that accompanied that was a lot of outrage from Christian conservatives in the United States who were upset that Bart was a bad role model for American children. My question at the time was, 'What comedy show has good role models?' If they're funny they're supposed to be silly or stupid in some way. But by Season 15 the worm had turned to the point where I was getting interviewed by and on the cover of Christian magazines because I [voice] Flanders and Lovejoy, as they realised that this was the only show on American television that had two avowedly Christian characters who go to church every week. So suddenly from having denounced the show, they were now embracing it.

On working with Michael Jackson for 'Stark Raving Dad':
He came into FOX to do the actual recording, and in those days there was a second read-through right before the recording. So we're sitting there around the table and Michael is doing his spoken words, but when it came to breaking into song, Michael sits back and this white guy on the other side of the table starts singing in a very Michael-Jackson-like voice. Nobody had explained any of this, so I turn to Yeardley Smith and I say, 'I think we paid enough for the talking Michael Jackson, but not enough for the singing one.'

On how he, Nancy Cartwright and Dan Castellaneta got cameos in the 1998 film Godzilla:

I think the producer was a fan of the show and thought it'd be cute to have people from *The Simpsons* in the film, so he convinced the director that it was a good idea.

On how he found the voice for Reverend Lovejoy:
I didn't base any voices on people I knew, except for at the end of the original season when they kept introducing new characters and I started running out of made-up voices. One of the last [characters] they added for me was Reverend Lovejoy, and there'd been this TV evangelist named Ernest Angley who would heal people. I did a piss-take of him on a show I once did, so I had his voice in my head and I just slowed it down a little bit until he became Lovejoy.

On keeping a sense of realism with his characters:
I think the funniest stuff going on is just observing real people. I don't try to make any of these characters that exaggerated, and I even cavil when they're written as doing things that I don't think they'd actually do if they existed. My touchstone is always to try and make them as real as possible.

On learning he has voiced at least 194 characters on the show:
I have not heard that number before, so I am actually bowled over. That's great, I'll be using that in the next negotiation.

Mitch's Top 5 Episodes

#5
'Simpson and Delilah'
(Season 2, Episode 2)

Homer scams his health insurance by charging $1,000 for the purchase of Dimoxinil, a new baldness cure. His miraculous hair growth leads to a happier life and instant promotion. Finding himself out in the cold, Smithers looks for a way to take Homer down and re-establish himself as Burns' right-hand man.

On the surface of things, 'Simpson and Delilah' may appear a left-field choice to find in my top 5 favourite episodes. It doesn't have a *lot* of jokes, the kids barely feature, and there isn't a sub-plot to keep wandering minds focused. It does, however, allow me to answer anybody questioning why it's so special with 'My reasons . . . are my own.'

This rags to riches to rags story explores Homer's insecurities, power dynamics in the workplace, and insurance fraud. It's a very adult episode, so naturally it's been one of my favourites ever since I was 4 years old. In fact, so important was this episode to my life that it is the sole reason for a lingering guilt that I still feel about the closure of my local video store some 21 years ago.

It was 1992, and the world was my oyster. Australia was

turning on one of its trademark summers. Beaches, cricket ovals and playgrounds everywhere were full of children, and I was making the most of it by spending as much time inside as possible. My mother took me down to the local Blockbuster on the first day of December, and with the pocket money I had saved, I rented a Simpsons video with a whopping two episodes packed into it. 'Simpson and Delilah', 'Treehouse of Horror'. I was an only child at the time, so I poured all the love normally reserved for siblings into that video, watching it ad infinitum until I knew every nuance of every scene. A lot happens in December, and the distractions of the holidays led my parents to forget about the video. One reminder came, then a second, then, not surprisingly, a third. Long story short, some miscommunication about whose back seat the video was on to take back to the store and a bitter divorce later, and suddenly I was an 8-year-old standing in front of a 'closed for business' sign wondering if this meant I would go to jail.

The premise of this episode is a simple one: Homer regrows his hair with the help of Dimoxinil. The details of how and why don't really matter to the enjoyment, which is a large part of why I was able to sit through it so many times as a kindergarten student. It's the feeling of desperation of Homer to seek a better life, and the sheer joy he experiences when he is no longer bald. After wishing everybody in Springfield a good morning, he checks straight into the barber's, as if he is making up for lost time. Homer sports a different haircut in every scene that follows. From a loose and ragged number that The Dude would be proud of, to a Gordon-Gekko-style power-do and everything in between. Underscoring the 'appearance is everything' mantra, Homer falls *up* the chain at work despite having shown no competency to do so. Hailed a hero by Burns simply because accidents 'have gone down by the number Homer Simpson is known or suspected to have caused himself', Homer is soon given the key to the executive bathroom. Ironically, the moment that Homer comes of age and delivers a brilliant speech, he is mocked and sent back to his own position on the grounds of his refound baldness.

The real joy of 'Simpson and Delilah' is, for me, one of the greatest guest characters of all time: the masculine yet effeminate Karl, played by Harvey Fierstein *(Mrs. Doubtfire, Independence Day)*. Karl is the guardian angel that everybody needs in their life. It's ironic that after overlooking all the secretary candidates who 'make kissy-faces' at him, Homer ends up employing a man who loves him instantly and deeply, and who literally kisses him later in the episode – a first for American television. Karl shows us a textbook example of how to nail a job interview, summing up Homer the moment he meets him as a fraud and a phoney. This isn't done out of nastiness, however. Everything Karl does is for the betterment of Homer. He drags him out of bargain basement lime-green polyester and into a suit that cries out 'Here I am, don't judge me, love me!' Later, when Smithers discovers Homer's insurance fraud, Karl throws himself on the grenade and bears its terrible brunt. I legitimately believe that Fierstein's performance taught me tolerance and acceptance. Is Karl homosexual or not? It's certainly implied, but what's more important is how little it matters. It taught me not to question somebody who comes off a little different, but to look at their motives instead. While the plot takes the cynical route, Karl still teaches confidence and self-belief. For a show that garnered controversy by pushing the envelope, 'Simpson and Delilah' is a beautiful piece of positivity, and an episode anybody should be happy to show to their 4-year-old children.

What did we learn?

Always save money for a rainy day.

#4
'Radio Bart'
(Season 3, Episode 13)

Using a microphone given to him as a birthday present by Homer, Bart convinces the town that a boy named Timmy O'Toole has become stuck down a well. When the attention spirals out of his control, he tries to put an end to things, only to become stuck down there himself.

New York can mean a lot of things to a lot of people. It's one of the greatest cities I've ever visited, and for 11 days I enjoyed a brilliant honeymoon there with my wife. The best things about New York are the unexpected gifts. I mean, everybody knows that you will see the Empire State Building, or Times Square, but there's so much hidden between the cracks that you'll find things you never expect. Even still, it took me by complete surprise that it would offer me a greater insight and understanding of what was already one of my favourite *Simpsons* episodes.

A combination of the cold weather, five days of sightseeing and a non-existent hot water system in our hostel had taken its toll, resulting in a day of being confined to our bed, and not in the traditional honeymoon sense. Flicking through the channels available, I stumbled across a vaguely familiar black-and-white face. The actor was Kirk Douglas, the film *Ace in the Hole*. As I watched, it smacked me in the face that 'Radio Bart' was clearly influenced by the movie. So now, by osmosis, when I watch 'Radio Bart', I think of my honeymoon. For that alone, it has to make it into my top 5. The fact that it's a great episode in its own right is just an added bonus.

While *The Simpsons* has often featured elements of social satire, 'Radio Bart' is one of the few episodes to be entirely structured around it. As a result, it's an episode that has only improved with the benefit of hindsight. 'Radio Bart' holds a mirror up to society as only the best satire can. It asks questions of us and it points out our hypocrisies without ever becoming preachy. The episode makes fun of mass hysteria and (over)reaction as well as media hype in a way that might as well have been predicting the future. In an age of social media and 24/7 news cycles, this is one of the more prescient episodes of TV to have ever existed.

The early part is spent focusing on Bart's birthday, with the main theme for comedy being the disconnect between father and son. It's hard not to feel sorry for Homer here, as he is utterly convinced that Bart is going to love his present: The Celebrity Superstar Microphone (it *is* better than a label-maker). While Bart is initially uninterested in the idea of badly distorted singing over the AM band, he does discover the radio can be useful for making pranks. The show slips in a *War of the Worlds* reference as Bart convinces Homer that

Earth has been overrun by aliens. The sight of Homer charging through the house, rifle in hand, is one for the ages.

Bart soon starts ramping up his pranks. He tricks Marge into thinking Maggie can talk to her, and Rod and Todd into thinking God can talk to them. It almost feels like a natural progression when he lowers his radio into the well. To a 10-year-old boy, there's no way of knowing what is going to follow. The moment that Groundskeeper Willie hears the false cries for help, the episode kicks into full-blown satire mode.

Even when we see the positive sides of mob mentality in this episode, it is still laced with a touch of cynicism. When the entire town is racing to the well after the initial discovery, nobody really seems to be doing it out of any desire to help. Instead, it appears that voyeurism is the motivator. The desire to say, 'I was there.' Later in the episode when Homer and Willie are setting about digging Bart from the well, again the town races as one to the scene, although this time it feels like many of them aren't even sure why. 'A good old-fashioned hole-diggin,' suggests Jasper. Again, it seems that the motivator is less about helping, and more about just being involved in something bigger.

The most savage skewering is saved for the media and do-gooder celebrities. Krusty and Sting (fantastic in a memorable cameo) put together a 'Feed the World' style tribute song. They feel good and are praised in the media although it's very clear that none of this will help the situation. Krusty even points out that there won't be much left after the royalties, production cost, money for limos etc . . . What *is* left gets thrown down the well.

The media are depicted as fickle, ratings hungry merchants. They and other profiteers set up permanent camp at the well, until the public start to lose interest, at which point a squirrel looking like Abe Lincoln takes centre stage. The media giveth, the media taketh away. The episode also comments on how fickle we can be as a society, in that when a boy the town doesn't like as much is trapped, sympathy is lost. Tragedy is no match for feeling personally slighted, it would seem.

My love for 'Radio Bart' could be seen as a precursor to my eventual love for *South Park*, and almost feels like a prototype for what that show would become. It's a peak example of *The Simpsons* delivering a story full of substance without skipping on laugh-out-loud moments. I'll always be sending my love down that well.

What did we learn?
Sting is a good digger.

#3
'Itchy & Scratchy Land'
(Season 6, Episode 4)

After watching Itchy and Scratchy promoting their new theme park, Bart and Lisa demand to be taken there for their next family vacation. Eventually, the kids get their way, much to the chagrin of Marge, who had been planning a trip to a bird sanctuary. After a horrifying shortcut, the family arrive at Itchy & Scratchy Land. All seems fun at first, but when the robots start to attack the guests, The Simpsons are faced with a fight for their lives.

There are a lot of reasons to love *The Simpsons*. I love Season 1 for the way it redefines the nuclear family and its crude charm. I love Season 2 for the underlying heart behind the laughs and its many stories that aim to make you feel as much as laugh. I love Seasons 3 to 5 for the transition from that emotionally based comedy to breakneck-speed joke writing. Where you think *The Simpsons* peaked is totally subjective, but for me it was Season 5. That said, if I want to watch for high-concept plots and non-stop side-splitting laughter, Season 6 is where I'll turn to. I could very nearly pick out a top 5 made up of episodes entirely from this season: 'Bart's Comet', 'Homie the Clown', 'Homer Badman' – classics, each and every one, but above them, there's something special that keeps bringing me back to 'Itchy & Scratchy Land'.

John Swartzwelder has the writing credit here, but it was apparently an effort by the whole team. While the main plot is relatively thin, the subtext is dense. In having the family travel to Itchy & Scratchy Land, the writing team poke fun at family vacations, Disneyworld, and Michael Crichton's Westworld. They also sneak in references to Crichton's *Jurassic Park*, and Hitchcock's *The Birds*. Come to think of it, the final discovery of how to defeat the evil robots by using flash photography is remarkably similar to a final act revelation in the 2017 horror film, *Get Out,* proving yet again that the Simpsons have done everything. In amongst it all, they generated revenue for transport authority departments worldwide as fans rushed out to purchase 'Bort' vanity licence plates for their cars.

A potential roadblock to your enjoyment of 'Itchy & Scratchy Land' is that it relies on some degree of knowledge of theme parks to get a full understanding of the comedy. I was fortunate enough to have family trips to Australia's Gold Coast to visit theme parks such as Dreamworld and Warner Bros. Movie World as a child. I was unfortunate enough to live some 1,800 km from those theme parks in an age where flying machines were the domain of the businessman, so I too know the pain of ill-advised shortcuts 13 hours into a 24-hour car ride. No amount of time spent posing next to the Dog on the Tuckerbox or climbing up Big Pineapples can save you from Australia's flat, ever-stretching landscape.

Once the Simpsons arrive, every theme-park cliché is quickly checked off and skewered with startling comedic precision, from theme restaurants to thrill rides and parades every five minutes. On entering the park, the Disney Dollar is replaced with Itchy & Scratchy Money, which of course isn't accepted anywhere. There's so much joy in watching Homer get swept up in the moment of the world's lamest sales pitch to the tune of dropping $1,100 of the 'fun' currency. The animators do a great job of providing a sense of expansiveness to the park, not daunted at all by the need to create entirely new sets for the majority of the episode. It gives the park a feeling that you could be there for days and not see everything, a special effort in a TV show where things can normally feel constrained.

The more time the family spends in the park, wreaking havoc on unsuspecting mascots as only Bart can, the more the park transitions from Disneyland to Westworld. The latter's recent TV remake could serve to help this episode find a new audience in the younger generation who have grown up on the show post 2000 and may not have come across it before. Not stopping with one Crichton novel to parody, *Jurassic Park* references are littered throughout, including Professor Frink's revelation that chaos theory dictates that the park can't be controlled. In true Frink fashion, his prediction is off by 24 hours due to a miscalculation, and the destructions starts practically before he can finish his warning.

The mood change is an abrupt one, with the score quickly shifting to the dramatic. The image of dozens of robot Itchy and Scratchies taking deliberate and menacing steps towards the Simpsons has proper horror/sci-fi chops, as a well-timed commercial break helps ramp up the tension. The animation is brilliant again, as a full-scale flash-photography battle breaks out. Ultimately, Lisa's cool head and Bart's dry action hero wit are enough to prevail, but sadly, not enough to prevent Euro Itchy & Scratchy Land from financial ruin.

As jam-packed with laughs and thrills as any episode in the show's pantheon, 'Itchy & Scratchy Land' is as enjoyable as *The Simpsons* gets when it comes to pure escapism.

What did we learn?

Bort is a remarkably popular name. Bart, not so much.

#2
'Homer the Great'
(Season 6, Episode 12)

After having one of those mornings where nothing goes right, Homer notices that Lenny and Carl are getting it all better than him: better car park, better chairs, better evening plans. Curious, and a little jealous, Homer follows them to a meeting of the Stonecutters. Discovering he is entitled to membership due to Grampa being a member, Homer joins the secret society, later to be discovered he is the prophesised 'Chosen One'.

When I was about 11 years old, I discovered in passing conversation that my grandfather was a Freemason. I didn't know what it meant then, and I honestly couldn't tell you what it means now. All I know is that it felt special. There's something about secret sects and societies that piques the curiosity in all of us. That's why conspiracy theorists like David Icke can convince millions that the government is secretly run by a race of lizard-people. This is hardly a new phenomenon. I've grown up on these stories. The great Sir Arthur Conan Doyle would write classic tales of murderous cults for Sherlock Holmes to track down, and I would lap up every word. So, when my grandfather told me he was a Freemason, it was a huge deal. The following year, when I discovered what I thought was a rival faction known as the Stonemasons, I prepared for a full-scale war. Imagine my disappointment when I discovered they were simply tradesmen.

I think people like to imagine these sorts of groups running the world because it gives a reason why things go wrong in life. Case in point, when a pipe springs a leak in Homer's basement, there's nobody to blame. When traffic is so bad it takes him hours to get to work, and even then he has to park behind his own house and begin a long walk back to the plant, it's just bad luck.

There's nothing worse in life than impotent fury with nobody to direct it towards. Having a cult to blame can change that, or, as Homer sees in Lenny and Carl, maybe fix it. As they seem to have everything better, he is desperate to find out how. Lenny, great keeper of secrets, won't budge on giving up the information. Even telling Homer the secret exists is enough for him to be told to 'shhhuuuddddduuupp' by Carl.

Watching Homer stalk Lenny and Carl is one of my all-time favourite Homer moments, because his idea of sticking a leaking paint tin on the back of their car is one of the most intelligent schemes he's ever come up with outside of his alcohol delivery system as the Beer Baron. His attempt to spy on the group via the skylight, however, is less successful. To repurpose Jim Carrey's line in *Batman Forever*, their entrance was good, his was worse. It should be noted that, given the size of the building, and the sheer number of citizens who are members, it probably should have been discovered prior to now . . . but I digress.

While a solution to life's trivialities is a perk for Homer joining the Stonecutters, for him, it's more about a general acceptance. For anybody who has ever felt on the outside of a club looking in, or feeling like the only person in the room who didn't get a joke, it's a nice way to contextualise Homer's desire to join the club. Once he does manage to gain access, for a moment he is genuinely accepted. The usual power dynamics are flipped about, as Mr. Burns is an underling to Lenny and Carl. These are the strongest scenes of the episode, culminating with the Emmy-nominated 'We Do', a song that is impossible not to sing along to. To continue talking too much about these scenes would just break down into listing the things that make me laugh, but I do have to give special mention to the brilliance of the stone of shame/stone of triumph.

If you were to look at how *The Simpsons* influenced *Family Guy*, you'd need look no further than 'Homer the Great'. There's a litany of reality-breaking jokes packed into this episode, including the tangential conversation between Homer and Lenny about cholesterol in eggs, followed by a man running away *dressed* as an egg who had evidently been spreading egg propaganda. Another classic is in the frat-house-style Stonecutter initiation, where Homer falls through five storeys of floors. Non-sequiter comedy like this can be so hit and miss, and incredibly subjective, but for me this is an example of the very best of it. It's hard to really explain or define; for all the words we will write in this book, it's just funny cos it is.

When I was in my early twenties, my grandparents came over to the house for a coffee. We watched 'Homer the Great' together as it happened to be on. As we laughed together, I thought about how it was such a treat to sit down and close a 50-year age gap with a cartoon. At the end of the episode, I brought up my memory of finding out that my grandfather was a Freemason.

'Stonemason, Mitch. I was a stonemason.'

'But . . . I thought you said . . .' I started, confused. Then, leaning in to me with a wink, he whispered, 'It's a secret.'

On cue, my grandmother, Dotty, looked harshly at him and said, 'Shhhhuuuddddduuupppp.'

What did we learn?

A secret handshake can get you an awful lot in life.

#1
'You Only Move Twice'
(Season 8, Episode 2)

Homer is offered a new job for Globex Corporation and packs up the family to move to Cypress Creek. On arrival, Homer finds his life greatly improved. He's good at his job and he loves his boss, supervillain Hank Scorpio. Oblivious as ever, Homer is thrilled with the move. The rest of the family have a hard time settling in, however, and ask for a move back home to Springfield.

In the final moments of 'You Only Move Twice', as Homer is reading a telegram from Hank Scorpio, he is told that 'Project Arcturus' could not have succeeded without him. For those unaware, Arcturus is the brightest star in the celestial northern hemisphere. Fitting, then, that this should be one of the brightest episodes in the history of *The Simpsons* and, in my opinion, a peak that was never reached again. Rather than a negative comment on the quality of the show since, it's the ultimate compliment to the quality on display here. I wanted to come up with a more creative choice for my favourite episode of all time, I really did, but I just *can't* bring myself to go past this one.

The law of diminishing returns can usually be applied to comedy, but with 'You Only Move Twice', the laughs are as big on the 100th viewing as they were on the first. This is a perfect example of an episode where no one character is the focus. It's not a 'Homer episode' or a 'Bart episode', it's a true 'Simpsons episode'. I'd always admired Larry David's ability to be able to write four individual storylines within the confines of a *Seinfeld* episode and tie them all together neatly at the end. It's an incredibly difficult balancing act, and it took the entire writing staff working together to execute it so flawlessly. Such is the strength of the boss-cum-villain, Hank Scorpio (Albert Brooks), that the inclination is to call this an all-time great due to him alone, but that would be to discredit the quality of everything else. From top to bottom, this is a truly perfect episode.

I don't think there's 22 minutes of TV that have ever tattooed more quotes on my brain to be remembered for eternity. Most of those are attributable to the ad-libbing genius of Albert Brooks, who recorded a total of two hours' worth of dialogue for his role. Legend has it that Albert's improv was so good that Dan Castellaneta simply couldn't keep up. Albert would improvise dialogue and Dan would later come up with a response, only to find that when they re-recorded the scene, Albert had come up with completely new dialogue. It reduces Homer largely to monosyllabic grunts as Hank runs wild, but more than that, it keeps the viewer on their toes as well. If the actors on the show don't know what's about to be said, then how could we possibly have any idea? It gives the episode a feeling reminiscent of live television, where anything could happen at any moment. In a time when so much of television feels so structured, it stands out even more on rewatching.

From the opening minute, there isn't a moment of wasted time, as we commence with one of the best cold openings in the show's history. It's usual to see Smithers kissing up to Mr. Burns when he or others are in the room, but to watch him singing about him as he walks alone down the street is as delightfully pure as Smithers gets. I love that there's no ulterior motive to his affection, a fact underscored when he refuses to entertain working for anybody else. It turns out to be a fork in the road moment for Globex Corporation, as it moves down the ladder to Homer. One wonders if Smithers, more qualified in every way, could possibly have succeeded to the same extent as Homer. It takes a Homer-level moron to be able to both motivate a team and remain completely clueless as to their actual work; had Smithers agreed, Scorpio's reign would have ended before it began.

The trouble with Cypress Creek is that none of the rest of the family are able to keep their eyes closed. Everything seems perfect on the surface, but not too deep underneath it's a different story altogether. Marge discovers that perfection is the enemy of the housewife, Bart struggles to fit into a school where the students have their act together, and Lisa's walk through the woods offers the best visual metaphor for the town when an owl swoops down to kill a chipmunk moments after she has happily said hello to both. The lesson is clear – Cypress Creek is a beautiful town that deals in danger. Well, danger, and Tom Landry's hat.

Having grown up enjoying the wish-fulfilment fantasies that only James Bond can provide, 'You Only Move Twice' is to me what 'The Springfield Files' is to Dando. But what this provides that the movies never could is a chance to watch the villain win. And not only win, but relish winning and make us laugh while he's doing it. This shoe-farewelling, hammock-district-installing, flame-thrower-touting, sportscoat-trendsetting genius is pure evil, and yet I find myself wanting to work for him. I feel like if you could successfully keep your eyes closed to all the murder and mayhem, he would provide for quite a successful career. I, for one, would want to take that chance.

What did we learn?

You can successfully motivate a team with donuts . . . and the possibility of more donuts to come.

The Little Interview with Liz Climo

Liz Climo has worked on The Simpsons *since 2003 as an animation artist. She is perhaps best known for her comic series,* The Little World of Liz Climo, *showcasing an eye for whimsy and optimism that has led to her publishing several collections and frequently posts online. She is also a published children's author, famous for her Rory the Dinosaur series.*

The Seemingly Never-Ending Story is one of our favourite post-90s episodes, which was also one of the first you worked on. What do you remember about your beginnings on the show?
I was so excited/nervous when I started! One of my favourite memories is from my first day of work. I drove into the parking lot, and suddenly felt very embarrassed because I had a Homer sticker on my car. I figured I probably looked like a lame super-fan! But then, walking through the hall, I noticed all the *Simpsons* paraphernalia decorating all of the cubicles, and I realised I had nothing to be embarrassed about. The show's employees have so much pride for what they do, it's one of the things I love about working there.

What have been some of your favourite episodes to have been a part of?

Actually, 'The Seemingly Never-Ending Story' is one of my all-time favourites, too. I was always a huge fan of that book growing up, and it was a lot of fun drawing the 'Simpsonised' versions of those characters.

Which characters and locations do you most enjoy animating on the show and why?
I only really draw the characters. The backgrounds are all done by a separate team of background artists (thank goodness, because they do a beautiful job, and are much better with perspective than I am!) Milhouse is my favourite character to draw. His features are very round and dopey, which I love. I like drawing Maggie a lot, too.

You've said in the past that you grew up watching The Simpsons. *What's your earliest memory of the show?*
I remember watching the first episode and becoming instantly obsessed. I went to school the next day and asked all the other kids if they had also watched it, and they were basically like 'No, we're 8. We're not allowed to watch that sort of thing.' But, kudos to my parents, because that early exposure is probably responsible for my career!

You seem like such a positive person and it shines through in your comics. How important is keeping a positive mindset when working in a job that requires creative thinking?
Thanks! I think it's important because the show has been on for such a long time, it's easy to become a bit comfortable or complacent. I try to remind myself often how cool it is to be working on this show that I used to love so much as a kid.

Working for* The Simpsons *is something that most fans can only dream of. Was it what you expected it to be, going in?
I think the thing that stood out the most when I started working on the show is how so many employees also grew up watching the show. It's a very specific type of job in animation, and you have to understand the subtle humour that is important in a sitcom versus, say, a Saturday morning cartoon. Being familiar with the show really helps with that.

What are some of the key things you've learned while working alongside acclaimed animators such as David Silverman?
David in particular is very good at capturing a mood in a single pose, which is very important because it's easy for the life to get sucked out of a drawing after it's passed through several hands. Starting off with a loose, expressive drawing is crucial. I'm not very good at those, but I try!

Do you have a favourite animation sequence, either that you have worked on, or one that you have seen from the show?
I worked on the Bart skating naked sequence from the movie. That was fun!

If you are ever struggling, what are some of the key reference points you might look back on to get the creativity flowing?
Relationships are the most important thing, especially for what I do with my comics. If I'm ever struggling

with a joke or an idea, I try to just boil it down to a simple exchange that I may have heard in passing, and find inspiration from that. I've definitely learned a lot about that from my experience of watching *The Simpsons*.

You've mentioned relationships being important to your comics. What are some of your favourite relationships on The Simpsons*?*
I really like the relationship between Marge and Lisa. They're fundamentally so different from one another, but they're both very smart and still have that lovely mother/daughter bond that shines through.

Outside of The Simpsons, *are there any animated films or TV shows that serve as an inspiration to you?*
I really love Miyazaki movies (*Spirited Away, Howls Moving Castle, etc*). I just love how detail oriented they are, and how there's not necessarily a 'good guy' and 'bad guy' but a collection of characters who change and grow throughout the story. I think that sends a beautiful message, especially to children.

There are going to be people reading this who would have a dream to be where you are. Can you tell us about your journey to the show?
I just always loved drawing, I did it all the time. I studied animation a bit in college, but never graduated because I didn't get into the animation programme. I got a job on *The Simpsons* shortly afterwards, thanks to a combination of the help of a friend who worked there, hard work, and incredibly good luck.

What piece of advice would you give to young artists looking to get into the industry?
Keep drawing (life drawing, especially. It's so important for animation). Also, expect to be rejected at least a handful of times, but don't let that discourage you – we've all been through it! If you want to create your own content, then stay true to your style, even if you don't think it's any good. If it doesn't look exactly like what everyone else is doing, then you're on the right track (in my opinion, at least).

Paper and pencil, or digital screen and stylus?
Cintiq tablet, now. But I resisted it for as long as I could! Before that, it was a sharpie and paper.

You're stuck on a desert island that happens to have a particularly awesome home theatre system. What three movies are on the shelf?
Shaun of The Dead, *Moonstruck* and *Fargo*.

***What episode best describes a day of working on* The Simpsons?**
'22 Short Films About Springfield'.

Season 4 (1992-93)
In Conversation

MITCH: I get asked a lot what I think are the best seasons of the show. A lot of people will point to the entirety of the first nine seasons as being the best, but I try to mark a bit harder than that. It's all subjective, but for me, it's Seasons 4 to 6 as being the *absolute* peak. Just look at the first few episodes of Season 4: 'Kamp Krusty', 'A Streetcar Named Marge', 'Homer the Heretic'. All brilliant. If the first three seasons were a gradual evolution of the show, Season 4 was a quantum shift forward.

DANDO: Knowing that the show's producers were toying with the idea of turning 'Kamp Krusty' into a feature-length movie but ultimately decided against it feels like such a wasted opportunity.

M: That's been well documented, but oddly they ran short of time on that episode as it was, so a movie would have been a stretch. Perhaps they could have dedicated more screen time to the parents enjoying life without children and added a fleshed out sub-plot.

D: Surely that incredibly talented group of writers could have put together a story worthy of the big screen. Can you imagine the hype for a *Simpsons* movie being released in 1992? It would have been a defining moment for most of our childhoods, much like the events of 'Itchy & Scratchy: The Movie'.

M: Oh well . . . we'll always have *Space Jam*.

D: The show underwent a lot of changes this season. It was the last time the original writing staff worked together, their final hurrah being 'Cape Feare', which didn't air until Season 5 but was written at this time. Not only did the writing staff finish up, but showrunners Jean and Reiss both left to work on *The Critic* . . .

M: Which people will be happy to know didn't stink.

D: . . . the show was now animated by Film Roman instead of Klasky Csupo; even Sam Simon left at the end of the season due to creative disputes. It was definitely a change of eras.

M: Which coincided with a massive change in the direction of the comedy. People point to 'Marge vs. the Monorail' as the turning point, but insertions of 'unrealistic' comedy were already being planted, such as Krusty being repeatedly electrocuted in 'Lisa the Beauty Queen', or Homer springing back into the fire in 'Homer the Heretic'.

D: The real-life issues and family values were still there, but so was the elevator to nowhere. 'Marge vs. The Monorail' set a new precedent of what could and couldn't exist within the *Simpsons* universe and the writers wasted no time in exploring their new-found freedom. Suddenly it was fine for Homer to battle giant spiders in 'Duffless' or for snakes to become fans of Barry White's soothing vocals in 'Whacking Day'. Looking back, Season 1's 'The Call of The Simpsons' probably would have slotted in just nicely with this batch of episodes.

M: It's no secret that the biggest changes on screen were brought about by a massive injection of 'unrealistic' comedy. Conan O'Brien had an impact that most writers could only dream of. He might have only four official writing credits, but his influence went well beyond that.

D: Well, in 'Mr. Plow', it was Conan who thought it'd be funny for Homer to prevent his car from falling off the mountain by changing the dial on his radio.

M: That's exactly the stuff I'm talking about. He also created the character of Captain McCallister. Beyond that, I get the feeling he'd have lifted people around him to be better. Writers' rooms are typically boring, frustrating rooms to be in, but Conan's natural energy lifted everybody around him. I think he would have driven the confidence to chase what was funny, no matter how strange it might be.

D: Regardless of the newly established 'wacky' style of comedy, James L. Brooks' presence is still strongly felt as the show continued to dish up some absolute tear-jerking moments. Whether it's singing along to 'Raindrops Keep Falling on My Head' with Homer and Marge in 'Duffless', or being a fly on the wall as Maggie utters her first word, 'Daddy', it's the power of these moments that defines why this is the greatest show on television.

M: That sort of emotional investment is still what lifts these episodes above all imitators, whether or not people realise it. Take 'A Streetcar Named Marge', for example. On the surface, there's already a huge amount going on. There's a musical adaptation of a film adaptation of a play, which is jammed with jokes that anybody who has ever done amateur theatre will love. The songs are brilliant. There's Maggie's *The Great Escape* inspired shenanigans at day care. But at the core it's just a story about Homer finally finding a way to connect with Marge.

D: There was some controversy about 'Streetcar,' with the 'New Orleans' song as the opening number. The whole thing was blown out of proportion, all because a critic published the lyrics out of context before the episode aired.

M: The funny thing is, that song was supposed to be an homage to 'No Place Like London' from *Sweeney Todd*. It was never really intended to go out of its way to make fun of New Orleans.

D: Season 4's version of 'Homer at the Bat' came in the form of 'Krusty Gets Kancelled', bringing in a variety of guest stars in the hopes of spiking the rating.

M: The difference here is that by setting it in Krusty's world, it feels like a much more natural way to include a bunch of celebrity cameos.

D: I think I always enjoyed the latter more because I actually knew who the guest stars were. Sure, seeing Mr. Burns berate a bunch of major league players was fun and all, but that doesn't come close to environmentalist Bette Midler taking out the trash.

M: Or Hugh Hefner's bunny research institute. It also gave me a *very* misinformed view of who Johnny Carson was and what he was capable of before I'd ever seen reruns of his show.

D: The Red Hot Chili Peppers were also a surprise package for me, the way Flea yells 'Hey Moe!' as he enters the wrap up party gets me every time.

M: As great as the Peppers are, my favourite music moment comes from another episode this season, with Lisa on guitar in 'Last Exit to Springfield'. It's such a fantastic episode overall, and has some truly memorable moments, but her protest song, followed up with a flawless cover of 'Classical Gas', is the pick of the litter. I would like to take this moment to formally apologise to all buskers I've demanded this song from in the past . . . and all those I will demand it from in the future.

D: After three and a half seasons of working around the clock, the show offered up 'So It's Come to This: A

Simpsons Clip Show', an episode designed to reduce the workload of the staff.

M: There was a time when negotiations were pushing to have four clip shows per season.

D: Thankfully that never got off the ground. There's only so many times you watch Homer attempt to jump Springfield Gorge.

M: If there is, I'm yet to hit my limit.

D: As far as clip shows go, this is about as good as it gets, since it still manages to tell a genuinely interesting story. Bart's infamous April Fools prank and subsequent beer explosion is one of my favourite visuals from the earlier years.

M: Whenever they have done clip shows, it's made much more palatable by the amount of new content they insert to stitch the clips together.

D: The best thing about Season 4 is also the saddest, and it's how quickly Conan moved on.

M: It was always going to happen. As he has gone on to prove for years fronting his own show, he just had too much talent not to be a star.

D: It would be interesting to see what episode ideas he could come up with nowadays, assuming he's separated himself from the show for the last two decades. If there's anyone out there who could recapture the distinct genius of the show's earlier seasons it's him.

M: Given that they have had guest writers in the past, such as Ricky Gervais and Judd Apatow, I'm sure if Conan came calling they'd be more than happy to say yes. Until then, we will have to be content with him occasionally performing the Monorail song at public events.

'New Kid on the Block'
(Season 4, Episode 8)
Review by Dando

Bart falls in love with his new next-door neighbour, Laura Powers. As hard as Bart tries, he is unable to bridge the age gap and get her to take a romantic interest in him. When he finds out she has fallen for Jimbo Jones, he tries to block the two from getting together. Elsewhere, Homer fights a legal battle against an all-you-can-eat restaurant.

The beauty with writing this book has been that it's served as a reminder of just how much the show means to me. In preparation, I asked my work colleagues what their favourite episodes were, and to my surprise two of the five said 'New Kid on the Block'. Over time I'd seemed to have forgotten how great this episode was, but that discussion brought back a flood of memories from my childhood that hadn't existed in years. The charm of *The Simpsons* is that particular moments and episodes help rekindle you with the happier times of your youth. For me, none do this quite so well as 'New Kid on the Block'.

The first episode written by Conan O'Brien manages to combine the story of Bart's first love, the aftermath of a bitter divorce, as well as my all-time favourite Homer sub-plot. In fact, I'd almost go as far as to say that Homer's 'David vs. Goliath' battle with The Frying Dutchman is my favourite Homer story, period. As ridiculous as his lawsuit may seem, Homer was well within his rights to challenge Captain McCallister's (making his first appearance) idea of All You Can Eat. He needed to do it, not just for himself, but for all of us. After all, 'that could've been me!' As I write this I realise that I could base my entire review around Homer's story alone, so let's just put it on the back burner for the time being and focus on the episode's main plot.

I like to call this Conan's forgotten episode. Whenever people are discussing his contribution to the show, 'Marge vs. the Monorail' and 'Homer Goes to College' are usually the topics of conversation, which is perfectly understandable given how special they are. However, while their fast-paced wacky plots paved the way for a new era to the show, 'New Kid on the Block' proved that Conan also knew how to tone it down.

Bart's infatuation with his new neighbour Laura Powers (played to perfection by Sara Gilbert of *Roseanne* fame) was a story that resonated with me as an 8-year-old, for I too had a crush on the older girl next door. Much like the tomboyish traits of Laura, my neighbour was the only girl I knew who enjoyed video games, except her specialty wasn't 'Escape from Death Row', it was 'Wonder Boy' on the Sega. After seeing these similarities unfold on my television screen, I honestly remember believing that this episode must have been written about me, and me alone. It was the first time I truly connected with the show on a personal level: this wasn't just funny, it actually meant something.

Your first crush is a pivotal moment in your life. It's a feeling that hits you out of nowhere and leaves you confused as to how to handle it. Lisa had already experienced hers with Mr. Bergstrom (and to a lesser extent Corey), but up until now the idea of liking girls was never on Bart's agenda. It was only nine episodes ago that he was belittling his best friend Milhouse for having a girlfriend, so to think he had suddenly become everything he'd always hated was truly a directional change in the character's development.

Having Bart search for advice from the two key male role models in his life was certainly a nice touch. Although he normally confides in Otto for school-related issues, this was far too personal, and there's no way Bart would ever want Otto knowing he was interested in a girl in the first place. Approaching Grampa and Homer added a sense of realism to Bart's curiosity and opened the door to one of my favourite Homer flashbacks as a child, the one where the monkeys are 'killing each other', which is also the first adult gag on the show that I can remember understanding. Then as I got older I found the scene that followed to be far more entertaining, when we get another piece of classic Homer parenting as he compares women to kitchen appliances and alcohol.

As much as this is a Bart-centric episode, Homer will always be the star as far as I'm concerned. The sheer desperation to get back to his table to finish his plate of food after being ejected from the restaurant is something I aspire to. Castellaneta's delivery of 'but the sign said all you can eat?' perfectly expresses both Homer's sadness and confusion, like a child being told he can't have a second bowl of ice cream. Thankfully Lionel Hutz comes to his rescue, the only time I can remember him winning a case.

The way Conan pulled a much-loved recurring gag from left field to help resolve the episode's main story was pure genius. We all get a kick out of Bart's prank phone calls to Moe, but the idea of Moe finally getting his revenge was even more tantalising. Granted, the fact that Bart was willing to let Jimbo be brutally murdered with a rusty knife for a crime he didn't commit may have been a step too far. Still, upon first viewing it definitely made for an edge-of-your-seat conclusion to a rather simple story of unrequited love.

'New Kid on the Block' will never be as iconic as Conan's other work on *The Simpsons*, but that doesn't stop it from being a real 'coming of age' moment for Bart. He no longer feared cooties and was willing to start putting himself in a vulnerable situation for a chance at love. Now all he had to do was grow a bad teenage moustache.

What did we learn?

A woman is a lot like a refrigerator.

'Marge vs. the Monorail'
(Season 4, Episode 12)
In Conversation

After a $3,000,000 windfall, Springfield must decide what to spend their money on. A travelling salesman convinces the town to build a new monorail, but is revealed to be a con-man whose shoddy craftsmanship and cheap materials have left a trail of destruction in his wake. The town just better have a damn good conductor.

MITCH: Of all of Conan O'Brien's contributions to *The Simpsons*, this is the most loved and influential. It marks a paradigm shift in the style of comedy that would be portrayed for the next several seasons.

DANDO: Conan has gone on the record as saying that this is his favourite episode that he wrote for the show. Apparently, it still gets brought up regularly during interviews to this day, but you can tell he doesn't mind since he seems genuinely proud of it, and so he should be.

M: You could easily argue that, despite his short run, Conan had as much influence on *The Simpsons* as any writer in the show's history, including James L. Brooks, Matt Groening, John Swartzwelder, etc. Up until this moment very little would happen that wasn't within the bounds of reality, but from this point on, anything was possible.

D: You can imagine there would have been a real contrast of styles at the writers' retreat that year. Al Jean and

Mike Reiss had kept the show firmly grounded in reality until then, under strict orders from Groening of course, so you can understand their hesitation when Conan first pitched the story to them. The idea that Groening would allow guest star Leonard Nimoy to beam out in the show's closing shot would have seemed laughable at the time, so it must have been a massive but relieving shock when he gave it the green light. That one decision opened up so many possibilities, setting a precedent for a new dynamic that the show had yet to explore.

M: And, as a non-*Star Trek* fan, introduced me to Leonard Nimoy.

D: Interestingly, Nimoy wasn't the writer's first choice to be the guest star. But now it's hard to imagine the episode without him. He completely bought into the insanity that he was a part of, delivering some of my favourite lines in the whole episode. He won me over the moment he leaned out of the monorail and saved Krusty from certain suicide because 'the world needs laughter'.

M: You could almost say that this was to *The Simpsons* what 'The Marine Biologist' was to *Seinfeld* in terms of stretching the bounds of reality while winning over fans, and yet Yeardley Smith has said that she, along with other cast members, absolutely hated the episode. I can understand why they felt that way about 'Homer at the Bat' with its use of excessive guest stars, but what wasn't there to love here? If anything, it breathed fresh air into the series and arguably played a key role in its ability to still be on the air almost 25 years later.

D: Maybe it was just too big of a shift for what they were used to, or hard for them to imagine during the table-read. The episode had the most absurdly perfect bookends, kicking off with Homer's rendition of *The Flintstones* intro and ending with the popsicle-stick skyscraper, giant magnifying glass and escalator to nowhere.

M: Conan has a great knack for writing visual comedy, and the animators support him brilliantly with their execution of Homer sliding along tubes and flying out a window to land in his car in that opening sequence. You can just imagine how exciting this episode would have been to draw because they got to do so much that they'd never done before. It would have been a nightmare, for sure, to create a top-down layout of Springfield for the Monorail to zoom around in, but you just get the sense that everybody involved had an extra level of excitement about the new possibilities on offer.

D: It was as if Conan felt like he might never have such comedic freedom in another episode, so he tried to cram in as much ridiculousness as possible. Even the fade to black as we continue to hear people's screams as they plummet from the escalator is genius. The episode literally leaves you laughing at people killing themselves.

M: That surreal comedy ramps up after the opening sequence as we see Burns and Smithers dumping toxic waste barrels in a park. In the past that joke might have still been included, but there's no way it would have been followed up with a mutant tree come to life and a laser-eyed squirrel.

D: What's amazing about this episode is that the jokes never get old upon repeat viewing. Whether it's the giant pothole filled with popcorn, the exploits of Mr. Snrub or even Sebastian Cobb's realisation that a haircut may have been unnecessary in the midst of a crisis, not a moment is wasted when it comes to delivering laughs.

119

M: Another great strength to the episode is that while it introduces a lot of reality-bending comedy, it doesn't exclusively rely on it. The writing itself is whip-smart. I particularly enjoy the back and forth between Wiggum and Quimby, arguing over who had the authority in the situation. If you work in politics and you haven't at some stage said to an opponent, 'Run along, Quimby, I think they're dedicating a phone booth somewhere' then I'm afraid you are letting your country down.

D: Bart's admiration for Homer was also a nice touch, since he doesn't get many opportunities to be proud of his father. Obviously Lanley selected Homer for the job purely at random, however Bart doesn't need to know that. In fact, he almost becomes Homer's little sidekick as a result, tagging along in the front cabin for the monorail ride. This allowed for some great banter, particularly their moment of reflection that it seems they're doomed to crash, but at least they'd be taking a lot of innocent people with them.

M: Of course, the show's centrepiece is a toe-tapping number that has gone down in history as a song that transcends the adoration of both hardcore fans and casual viewers alike.

D: I don't think there's a *Simpsons* fan alive who can read the word 'monorail' in non-chorus fashion. 'The Monorail Song' is such a fun jingle that really encapsulates the enthusiasm Conan brought to the writing room.

M: To give an idea of how catchy that song is, there's something that hadn't really occurred to me until now. As obvious as this sounds now, $3,000,000 isn't really a lot of money in the scheme of a city budget. The Las Vegas Monorail cost something like $650,000,000 for only 4.4 miles of track. Considering that, maybe fixing

120

Main Street, or even investing in Bart's killer ant-bots, was a much more realistic option.

D: I'd never thought about that before, but as a taxpayer I'd have to agree.

M: Of course, a budget line and logic can't compete with a catchy jingle from a confident salesman. 'The Monorail Song' stands clear at the top of the *Simpsons'* impressive catalogue of musical numbers. I can't open a canned food item without starting to sing it in my kitchen.

D: When it comes to one-time characters, very few are more memorable than Lyle Lanley. You'd have to think Conan wrote the role with Hartman in mind since the man was such a comedic genius. With his sharp wit and charming demeanour, Lanley is the smooth talker Hutz always dreamed he could be.

M: Lanley may be a fraud, but he's a brilliant salesman. Even when being grilled by Lisa, he manages to distract her with flattery by playing to her intelligence. He has an answer for everything. It puts him up there with the best fictional con-men. I like to imagine an alternate universe where he hatches schemes with the guys from *The Sting*.

D: Ironically, Lanley unwittingly chose the one person in town who would have been able to stop the monorail . . .

M: What I love about Homer here is that he remains completely oblivious about how bad he is. He genuinely believes that he's a great conductor, and he takes pride in it. But, as you say, a legitimately qualified conductor probably could not have managed to stop the monorail whilst simultaneously separating conjoined twins.

'Brother from the Same Planet'
(Season 4, Episode 14)
Review by Mitch

Bart joins up to the Bigger Brother programme in an act of revenge after Homer forgets to pick him up from soccer practice. At first oblivious to his son's actions, Homer soon discovers what Bart is doing with his time, and in a fit of jealousy he joins the programme himself. Meanwhile, Lisa fights a crippling addiction to The Corey Hotline.

'Brother from the Same Planet' excels in combining the very best elements of *The Simpsons* into one neat package. It has a perfect mix of the reality-distorting comedy that was by now making its way into more and more episodes, such as the flying nun literally exploding on impact after being swept away by a storm. It has plenty of sweetness in Pepi and, to an extent, in Lisa's battle to stop calling the Corey Hotline. It is also jam-packed with movie references and has some of the greatest non sequiturs of all time, including Homer's infamous argument with his own brain when listing his motivation for joining the Bigger Brothers ('Don't say revenge').

In pitting Homer against Bart, 'Brother from the Same Planet' sets up a brilliant rivalry between the show's two most prominent characters. The two have had moments of not seeing eye to eye in the past, and Homer's role as authority figure has positioned him as a roadblock in Bart's way, but we haven't seen them scheme and plot against each other like this before. As a movie buff, the opening sequence of Bart waiting for Homer almost feels like it was written specifically for me. Bart communicating via Milhouse to 'trab pu kcip' à la *The Shining* is the highlight, while the joke about the kids sneaking into an R-rated movie that turns out to be *Barton Fink* is another great example of a joke that I didn't get until I was much older. Maybe I'm not giving Milhouse & Co. enough credit, but I'm not sure that the critically acclaimed film from the Coen Brothers that contains no sex or violence isn't what they had in mind.

Homer's unique ability to be oblivious to any situation is in full force, as his environment is virtually screaming at him to pick up Bart. Marge literally reminds him before leaving the house and thinks he has taken it on. If only the *Wheel of Fortune* answer had been 'What was that, honey?' Not even the retirement of Green Bay legend 'Bart' Starr is enough to kick Homer into action. It's not until he decides to take a bath that it hits him. To his credit, once he has realised that he is several hours late, he wastes no time on trivialities such as clothing when racing out the door. The 'acting' from Bart when Homer picks him up is quite something. The animation/direction deserves all the credit as Bart conveys a silent fury that somehow holds up even as a spilled sundae slowly melts on top of his head. As visual jokes go, it's as good as they come. Further conveying his rage, he imagines Homer's face melting and a world on fire in a scene reminiscent of *Terminator 2: Judgment Day.*

While watching Krusty host *Tuesday Night Live* (writer Jon Vitti's parody of *SNL*, where he previously worked) Bart sees an ad for Bigger Brothers. Bart's eventual bigger brother, Tom, was written with Tom Cruise in mind. There are numerous references to Cruise's films, as Tom rides a motorbike and is an F-14 pilot for the Navy. It's hard to imagine a bigger guest star this side of Michael Jackson than Tom Cruise in 1993, and I'll go to my grave wondering what kind of energy he would have brought to the character. But, as Scientology teaches us, when one door closes a window is opened on Xenu . . . or . . . something. In any case, Phil Hartman – a frequent guest as Hutz or Troy McClure – took the role of Tom and made it his own. It's such a treat to be able to watch him play a character central to the plot. When he introduces himself at the school with his larger than life voice and tosses Bart a personalised motorbike helmet, it inspired 5-year-old Mitch to race into the shed and paint lightning bolts on his own helmet.

Not to be forgotten, Lisa and Marge face their own battles, but unlike Bart and Homer, they tackle it together. It makes sense that an isolated 8-year-old would seek companionship in the pre-recorded messages from her teen idol. Like any addict, Lisa struggles to get dry, but is able to do it with the support of those around her. This sub-plot is most notable for the inclusion of the Skinner *Psycho* parody, with Mother's watchful gaze and swift hand an ever-present spectre looking down on the school. Skinner identifying a 900 number shows how skilled this Principal is at identifying misbehaviour and budget expenses.

A great set-up to a story is nothing without a great

conclusion, and the epic battle of Homer and Tom certainly delivers. Fighting all over Springfield, down and back up the gorge, into and out of antique stores, it's a fight akin to the climax of the first *Iron Man* film. Homer gives it his best shot, but the final wince-inducing 'crick' as his back is bent over a fire hydrant may as well be the final bell in this encounter. It's fitting that Bart, who started everything, is the one to fix up Pepi with Tom. It alleviates any guilt Bart was feeling for taking up a bigger brother when he didn't really deserve it. It's also nice to see Bart realise that while Homer may not be the perfect father, he's the perfect father for him. You can choose your bigger brothers, but you can't choose your family.

What did we learn?

To shake your booty means to wiggle one's butt.

Trivia Challenge

1. How much weight did Homer have to gain to be qualified as disabled?

2. Who teaches the orange eating class at the Adult Education Annex?

3. What food is at the top of Dr. Nick's 'Nutrition Pyramid'?

4. How long was Krusty estranged from his father?

5. Who is the Springfield A&M mascot?

6. How many screens does Mr. Burns have in his office?

7. What number Stonecutter is Mr. Burns?

8. Where does Skinner first kiss Mrs. Krabappel?

9. What is Freddy Quimby's licence plate?

10. Which characters are on The Home Wreckers bowling team?

11. What happens to Skinner when he gets upset?

12. Which Mexican wrestler do The Investorettes sponsor?

13. What is the name of the bootleg adults-only Itchy and Scratchy cartoon?

14. How much does Chester J. Lampwick sue Roger Myers Jr. for?

15. How many television channels does Springfield have?

16. What medical condition does Sideshow Mel have?

17. What was Barney holding at the NASA press conference?

18. How many girls are on Springfield pee-wee football team?

19. Where does Lisa find the secret confession of Jebediah Springfield?

20. What model is Homer's auto-dialler?

21. What did Bart take a bite out of at Freddy Quimby's birthday?

22. What year did Marge graduate high school?

23. How many members were there originally in the Flying Hellfish?

24. Where is Leon Kompowsky from?

25. How many times has Nelson seen *Itchy & Scratchy: The Movie*?

26. What was Moe's original boxing nickname?

27. According to Mr. Burns, what three demons must you slay to succeed in business?

28. How much is the Springfield Bear Patrol tax?

29. What colour is Poochie's hat?

30. What is KBBL's frequency?

31. Who steals Mr. Burns' trillion-dollar bill?

32. How much does Bart pay for the *Itchy & Scratchy* cel?

33. What bridge does Hank Scorpio blow up?

34. What year did someone first make jokes about Giant Handed Man?

35. Who runs the Ajax Steel Mill?

36. How much does Homer charge to see the 'angel'?

37. What award does Lisa envision impaling Bart on?

38. What business does Homer try to reach with a stick in New York?

39. What is the name of the baby with one eyebrow?

40. What is the title of Lisa's 'Patriots of Tomorrow' essay?

41. Which NHL player did Bart pass off as Woodrow?

42. What does Homer's shirt say in the continuous loop video?

43. What does Nelson always bring to show & tell?

44. Where was Sideshow Bob hiding at the air show?

45. What is the Dean's name in *School of Hard Knockers*?

46. What does Marge buy with the money from Homer's swear jar?

47. What were Kent Brockman's winning lottery numbers?

48. How much is Bonestorm?

49. How much is a suitcase of beer at the Kwik-E-Mart?

50. What game do Cooder and Spud run at the Springfield Carnival?

51. What time do the mob arrive for their pretzel money?

52. How many puppies does Santa's Little Helper father?

53. What town does Larry Burns live in?

54. What type of fruit tree did Lisa want in the backyard?

55. What Gladiator is Luanne Van Houten's boyfriend?

56. What drink does Grampa order at La Maison Derrière?

57. Where was Homer heading when he had to stop over in New York?

58. What is the title of Mr. Burns' autobiography?

59. What animal is the mascot of Shelbyville's football team?

60. Which band steals from Peter Frampton?

61. What is the name of Bart and Lisa's Itchy & Scratchy cartoon?

62. How many quarters does it cost Milhouse to play the Waterworld arcade machine?

63. What fake name does Bart give to Brad Goodman?

64. What does the Mr. Sparkle employee's shirt say?

65. How many numbers does Homer dial to call the Mr. Sparkle factory?

66. How old was Frank Grimes when he blew up in a silo explosion?

67. What does Skinner's BBQ apron say?

68. What do the Movementarians call their distant home planet?

69. Who leaves their glasses in the toilet at the power plant?

70. What does the sign say on the door to Apu's secret staircase?

71. How many times does Sideshow Bob step on a rake in 'Cape Feare'?

72. What two fruits do Bart and Nelson race on the school bus?

73. How many teeth are visible in Cletus' overbite?

74. What band does Bart think he sees in New York?

75. What was the title of The Be Sharps' second album?

76. What year did Sting use to open for Krusty?

77. What is the address Molloy says he buried the treasure at?

78. What store does Marge buy her Chanel suit from?

79. What product does Barney ask the pancake syrup for directions to?

80. How much does Moe pay for Krusty's bed?

81. What is Sideshow Mel's real name?

82. What is Homer's favourite flavour of donut?

83. How many consecutive hours did Apu once work at the Kwik-E-Mart?

84. How many glasses of water does Bart drink on Christmas Eve?

85. How long does it take Moe's deep fryer to flash-fry a buffalo?

86. Which episode featured 'The Adventures of Ned Flanders'?

87. How many atoms does Mr. Burns' grandfather find in the worker's pocket?

88. What's the first thing Lisa hears Malibu Stacy say?

89. How much does Homer originally charge for a ride on Stampy?

90. How many hours a day does Marge spend at home?

91. What show do Bart and Milhouse go see on their Squishee bender?

92. What episode did Itchy & Scratchy first appear in?

93. What song do Bill & Marty accidentally play on Valentine's Day?

94. Which football player gives Homer the Pigskin Classic game ball?

95. How powerful is the bomb Sideshow Bob steals at the air show?

96. What extra ingredient does Wiggum add to his chilli?

97. What painting does Bart wipe away whilst cleaning the house?

98. What does Comic Book Guy plan to watch while eating his 100 tacos?

99. Which Little Rascal did Moe kill?

100. Where was Lyle Lanley intending to fly to?

101. How many bathtubs does Homer buy to brew his own alcohol?

102. What did Krusty's memorial grave say?

103. What is the name of Nelson's soapbox racer?

104. What is the Mr. Plow phone number?

105. Whose grave does Homer mistake for his mother's?

106. Which Be Sharp plays the banjo?

107. What is Springfield's town motto?

108. What type of flower did Nelson pick for Shary Bobbins?

109. What is Flanders' room number at the Calmwood Mental Hospital?

110. What colour is Krusty's bowtie?

111. Who was Springfield's Sanitation Commissioner before Homer?

112. Who travels to space with Homer and Buzz Aldrin?

113. What was the first thing to ever go wrong at Itchy & Scratchy Land?

114. What team do the Pin Pals defeat first?

115. What's inside the former Knoxville Sunsphere?

116. How much did Homer spend on his dummy to get out of work?

117. Which celebrity did Homer miss out on meeting at the mall?

118. What is the name of Homer's internet business?

119. How much did Mr. Burns sell the Springfield Power Plant to the Germans for?

120. What is the name of cousin Merl's dog?

121. What was Lisa's first word?

122. Who is McBain's partner?

123. How much did Homer pay for Lisa's pony?

124. What does Moe do on Wednesday nights?

125. What colour is the novelty foam hand Smithers buys for Mr. Burns?

126. Who is the owner of the Shelbyville Power Plant?

127. How many hours did Lionel Hutz babysit Bart and Lisa?

128. What year did Roger Myers steal the rights to Itchy from Chester J. Lampwick?

129. What number jersey does Nelson wear for the Springfield Wildcats?

130. How much does Mr. Burns pay Krusty to deliver a pizza to Bart?

131. What are the names of the three nerds in 'Homer Goes to College'?

132. What pastry does Kent Brockman eat before reading the news?

133. On which site does Comic Book Guy find out who is playing Radioactive Man?

134. What mountain do Homer and Mr. Burns get trapped on?

135. What fake name does Bart use to purchase Laddie?

136. What is the secret ingredient of a Flaming Moe?

137. What episode did Disco Stu first appear in?

138. What colour was Rabbi Krustofski's hair when he was younger?

139. Where was The Simpsons 138th Spectacular held?

140. What is the name of Rancho Relaxo's masseuse?

An Interview with Mike B. Anderson

Mike B. Anderson has worked on nearly 400 Simpsons episodes in one role or another, doing everything from character layout to directing episodes. His directorial debut came in Season 7 with 'Lisa the Iconoclast'. Since then he has two Emmies for 'Homer's Phobia' and 'HOMЯ'.

You've directed several episodes featuring guest stars – Donald Sutherland, Willem Dafoe, John Waters et al. What are the differences or similarities in your approach to them compared to the regular cast?
Simpsons acting is the visual expression of the vocal performance. The script dictates staging and the voice track informs the acting. Our main cast delivers such vivid voice tracks that it's not hard to imagine the *Simpsons* characters' performances, especially since we've been animating them for 28 seasons. With guest stars, it's a kind of fresh start. Their voice performances have their own qualities and idiosyncrasies to consider. If they are playing a version of themselves, then it's cool to display the actor's traits, postures and iconic behaviours in their acting. I always want to study the guest celebrities' work and try to get it right. Even if they are doing a voice for an entirely new character, you can use their known traits to help realise the personality of that new character. For example, you can see a lot of Albert

Brooks in Hank Scorpio's personality. In all cases, the vocal performance is the great guiding force on how to animate the character.

'Homer's Phobia' was acclaimed at the time it went to air. Twenty years later, how would the episode change to reflect today's culture?
I don't think it would have to change. It's just as relevant and entertaining as it was 20 years ago! Obviously, the gay subject matter isn't as shocking today as it was in '97, but the story of prejudice between different kinds of people is timeless and is a perfect conflict for dramatic comedy. Bias is usually a negative trait in real life. The kind of bias in 'Homer's Phobia' is endearing because it's Homer . . . and because he ends up being tenderised by a herd of reindeer ramming him repeatedly.

It is said that film is a director's medium, television is a writer's medium, and stage is an actor's medium. Where does animation fit in?
On *Simpsons*, the script is the master and all efforts are to realise the vision of that script. That said, directing an episode is very much like directing a movie – you tell the story through acting and visually realising the details of the story in every way that a live-action director does.

How much direct influence do you have over an episode?
The animation director does have a big influence over the final episode and its overall effectiveness as entertainment. It's a big responsibility. Luckily, we have a great team of talented directors, who all worked their way up into that position by drawing thousands of

Homers, Marges, Barts, Lisas, Maggies and everyone else in Springfield.

Who would you say has been the biggest influence on the show in your time working there?
When I first started on the show in 1990, David Silverman was the guiding force of the *Simpsons* look and animation. He set the aesthetic style for the show with his Christmas Special, 'Simpsons Roasting on an Open Fire'. He was the guy who said, 'Don't draw it like that, draw it like this.' We had meetings about elbows, hair hoops, pupil sizes and everything. Every detail was decided upon and added to the style guide. No doubt David was funnelling Matt Groening's sensibilities into this guidance, but you can feel David's style in *The Simpsons*. Brad Bird also had a huge impact on the style of storytelling in the early days of *The Simpsons*.

How was Brad's approach different to that of the others?
Brad looked to classic movies for staging inspiration and wanted shots to be very narrative and cinematic – more like movies than television. The first director I worked for on the show was Rich Moore (*Futurama*, *Wreck-It Ralph*, *Zootopia*) and I learned a lot of animation tricks from him too – tricks I still use today.

What episode do you wish you could have made?
If you're referring to an existing episode that I didn't direct, but wish I had, I might say 'Homer's Enemy', not because I think I could do a better job (that was pure Jim Reardon and hilarious), but because I love the Frank Grimes character so much and it's one of my

favourite episodes. What I'd rather say is, I would love to direct another episode with John Waters that sees his 'Homer's Phobia' character return for another adventure with the Simpsons. I have some cool ideas for a plot and would love to make that happen. I think fans would love it too!

Do you think it's a possibility?
I'm friends with John and he tells me that, even though it's been 20 years, people still constantly talk to him about being on *The Simpsons*.

Is there an episode you wish you could have done differently?
I like all the shows I've directed, some better than others, but I do admit there's a few animation moments that make me cringe when I see them. In almost every case, it's because I ran out of time and feel I didn't really make a moment shine as well as it should have. Sometimes there's a small technical flaw that there was no time to fix, and that makes me crazy. The truth is, most viewers are never aware of these flaws because they're enjoying the story. (I won't help you by telling you which episodes I think have flaws.) We do these shows really fast for how ambitious they are, and at some point, they just have to be finished. *Simpsons* directors are notoriously schedule-challenged and try to squeeze in more time to make things better. It's because they all want to make their shows the best they can be, which drives them to revise scenes up to the last minute.

How has the process changed since you started?

Technically speaking, it's gone from the Stone Age to the Space Age. We still hand-draw all the characters, just not on paper. In the old days, everything was shot on film, which had to be processed overnight. If the animation was flawed or timed badly or just wrong, it would have to be shot again and wait another day for the retake to come back from the lab. Today, we draw on computer screens (Wacom tablets) and every artist has the software and ability to test the animation, refine the timing and add or subtract poses, then spit out a QuickTime movie to show the director. This could happen in hours, or even minutes, with endless possible revisions. The first 13 seasons of Simpsons production (1989–2002) were all drawn on paper, shot on film and finished on painted animation cels. I directed the last episode produced with animation cels, 'How I Spent My Strummer Vacation'. After that, the show was all digital ink and paint, done on computers. This opened up the colour palette too, and shows started becoming more sophisticated in their art direction. I personally like digital tools because you can fix things on the spot and adjust timing to be faster and funnier. The next big production shift happened in 2007, right after *The Simpsons Movie*, when the show went high-def and expanded to the widescreen (16:9) format.

As someone who has worked on the show for its entire journey, during which period would you say your job was the most challenging?
It's all relative. Producing *Simpsons* shows is always challenging, but I think the early paper and cels days were a little harder than it is now with computer tools.

I like the flexibility of computers to improve animation on the spot and retime things to be more effective. Then again, the writers are aware of these advantages and so they write bigger scenes with bigger crowds and parades and events that occur everywhere on earth. It keeps it interesting, but the scope of the stories has been enlarged to fit the advantages and so I suppose it's a toss-up on the amount of work. In the history of production, one unusual challenge stands out above others – the North-ridge earthquake in 1994. We were finishing Season 5 and just starting Season 6 when the quake hit early on a Monday morning. The building where we worked was deemed unsafe and so the whole production was displaced. Small batches of people were allowed inside the building to gather the drawings and materials so they could set up temporary workspaces in nearby, undamaged buildings. There were several weeks when we worked almost shoulder to shoulder to keep the shows in motion. A couple of directors set up shops in their garages at home and had their teams work there. The show must go on . . . and it did.

Martin Scorsese has Leonardo DiCaprio. Christopher Nolan has Michael Caine. Who is your favourite actor to work with?
The main cast always dazzle with their performances and I've had wonderful experiences animating all of them. Lisa singing for 'The President Wore Pearls' felt incredibly special. I certainly love working with all Dan Castellaneta's characters. He's just plain funny. Sometimes at table-reads (the first read-through of a new script), Dan might have to do a conversation between

138

Homer, Grampa, Krusty the Clown and Willie – all Dan voices – and it's hilarious to see him juggle voices and personalities. A personal favourite – I've had the privilege of working with Albert Brooks' voiced characters many times, including in *The Simpsons Movie*, and each time has been fantastic.

What were some films that influenced 'Halloween of Horror'?
I'm a big fan of horror and sci-fi movies so I was very excited when supervising producer, Matt Selman, said he wanted it to be scary. There are nods to many classic horror icons that horror buffs know well – *Halloween, Alien, Night of the Living Dead, Texas Chainsaw Massacre*. I researched an old favourite, *Lady in a Cage*, for the home invaders' demented personalities. I also went and experienced the Universal Halloween Horror Nights event (which was really scary) for insights to do Krustyland Halloween Horror Night. My proudest moment was watching the episode with my daughter and having her tell me how scary it was to see the three scuzzos' reflections in the kitchen window.

What excites you more – a blank piece of paper, a storyboard, or a finished product?
I really enjoy the whole process. It's all about solving problems – story problems, staging problems, art problems. One of the more brain-sizzling fun activities is the bi-weekly, all-day, storyboard review process, where we analyse the rough storyboards of an entire episode. We tear them apart, add and delete shots, improve staging, make jokes work better, combine shots, add more

cinematic angles, inject new ideas, etc. It's an intensely creative meeting that takes an entire day, and sometimes two, depending on the complexity of the episode. Good ideas are mined from all the participants. It's exhausting but very rewarding and a lot of magic happens.

Some people have suggested a potential for the show to start creating topical shorts for the YouTube generation. Do you see a future in this medium for the show?
Simpsons recently produced humorous shorts for online consumption lampooning President Trump. That could be considered topical. *The Simpsons* tends to explore and experiment with all new formats and media when they appear, but I don't know that being topical is on the agenda. My personal feeling is that if *Simpsons* has something topical it wants to comment on, then it will. We have certainly proved that we can produce an animated piece on a moment's notice.

The episode 'You Only Move Twice' is highly regarded by viewers as one of the greatest episodes in the show's history. Did it have the same appeal from a director's perspective?
'You Only Move Twice' was the second episode I directed and it really felt like something special when we were making it. I was (and am) a total Albert Brooks fan boy, so the chance to animate a character with his voice was a rock star moment for me. We had six weeks to produce the animatic in those days (which is a rough, posed out version of the show for the producers to scrutinise and rewrite). Hank Azaria had performed all of Scorpio's lines at that point; quite brilliantly, actually.

Three weeks into our process, we got the Albert Brooks voice track and it was maybe 75% different from the scripted lines (Brooks was famous for his ad-libs and improv). This meant we had to restage a large portion of the Scorpio performance, with only three weeks to dead-line . . . His voice was so awesome, we just did it and had a great time doing it. The Scorpio character was so well received by the producers, they trusted me to direct the next Halloween episode, 'Treehouse of Horror VII'. Had a blast with that one too. I love my job!

***Which unique qualities do you think you bring to the table when directing an episode of* The Simpsons?**
I believe I'm a good storyteller with a knack for finding the funny in any situation. It's a good fit for directing *Simpsons*, which is loaded with hilarious dialogue and story situations that must be staged to realise both the story and humour. It helps that I have been blessed with some amazing scripts. I was elated to get the 'Trilogy of Error' directing assignment. I loved the puzzle quality of the idea and juggling all the details to make the premise work. It was much harder to make the idea work than it might look. A funny side note – the producers told me that 'Trilogy of Error' was their choice as the episode they wanted to put up for the Emmy award that year. I was very happy until I later heard they had decided on a different episode. Oh well. That's the way it goes . . . Then I heard it was 'НОМЯ' they chose instead and I was happy again. 'НОМЯ' ended up winning the statue that year.

What episode best describes working on the show?

At this point, 'Future-Drama' comes to mind (which I also happened to direct). No one could have predicted the future of this little show when it first aired in December of 1989. The world is such a different place than it was 28 years ago. Public tastes have changed and evolved. Huge technological advancements and new media have distracted and splintered audiences in different directions. So many other TV shows have come and gone. But *The Simpsons* is still here, and it's hard to imagine a world without it or what future drama will finally lead to the last episode being produced. I'm positive that even after the series wraps, whenever that is, *The Simpsons* will be with us in ways that we can't predict. Maybe not the answer you were looking for, but that's what popped into my head.

Note: I'm sure some of my responses are perhaps a little too reverent to *The Simpsons*. I can't help it – I love this show so much. I often marvel at its long history and ponder all the things that had to happen just right, and not to happen wrong, for a TV show to survive almost three decades of world events and still be popular. Maybe *The Simpsons* is just that special. I feel incredibly lucky to have been in the right place at the right time to win a job that I'm still excited about 28 years later.

Dando's Backstage Tour

When I asked my wife to marry me six years ago, I never imagined that our honeymoon would include a tour of the *Simpsons* animation studios.

I must begin by thanking *Simpsons* production supervisor Nikki Isordia for organising it all; without her this opportunity never would have happened. In fact, a lot of Four Finger Discount's success would have never eventuated had it not been for Nikki's generosity. This experience wasn't something I asked for, rather it was a special gift that she offered and for that I will be forever grateful.

Waiting by the front of the building with both my wife Nicola and one of my best friends, Matt (who was conveniently in the US at the same time), I found myself thinking back to 'The City of New York vs. Homer Simpson' when Bart found *MAD* magazine's HQ. Standing outside those doors, I was just as nervous and excited as he was. Even Nicola, who is by no means a diehard fan of the show at all, was thrilled with excitement. How could we not be? We were about to visit *The Simpsons*!

To look at the building, you would never know that this is the home of the greatest animated series of all time. Unlike the famous FOX lot, there are no murals featuring our favourite characters sprawled across the exterior – it appears to be just another office building in the concrete jungle of Burbank, California. Admittedly, things may have changed since, as they had only moved into the building a few months prior to our visit.

Upon being greeted by Nikki and her puppy/best friend, Bowie, who has somewhat taken the role of an office mascot, the time had finally come. As we began making our way upstairs, I immediately became stricken with the fear of embarrassing myself in front of all these people who I respected so highly. A part of me kept thinking: How should I introduce myself? What should I ask? *Should* I ask anything at all? Will they even care? Meanwhile, the other part of me was wondering why the animation studio of one of television's biggest icons was merely just another level of a multi-storey complex. Disappointingly, their floor wasn't even wedged in between bowling alleys.

As we entered the reception area we were greeted with a beautiful mural of the opening shot of the intro, with the words 'The Simpsons' in front of a cloudy sky. I've only squealed with glee a handful of times in my life, and I'm not ashamed to admit that this was one of them. Gazing around the wide-open room, I felt like a child about to visit Disneyland for the first time. Offices surrounded a hub of cubicles that were filled with *Simpsons* sketches and memorabilia. I felt a sense of satisfaction knowing that I collect the same *Simpsons* paraphernalia as the people who create the show themselves. From the World of Springfield action figures to a Super Nintendo cartridge of Virtual Bart, this was a museum of *Simpsons* nostalgia. It actually had a calming effect on my nerves as I realised that these incredibly talented people are all fans, just like you and me.

Whilst Nikki was giving us a brief tour to start the day, I was busy trying my hardest to appear invisible as I peeked over the shoulders of animators at work. Watching a professional draw these beloved characters with such ease was a thing of beauty. As Bowie continued to lead us down the hallway I remember getting distracted by a storyboard and walked right into a cubicle wall. The beauty of lagging behind at the back of the pack is that nobody notices when you make a fool of yourself. After a brief visit to Nikki's office the tour ended with an unexpected stop at the office of acclaimed director, Rob Oliver. 'He's the guy who designed the covers of the DVDs!' I whispered to my wife with excitement.

As we all took a seat in Rob's office, Nikki suddenly left for a meeting. I immediately had flashbacks of my mother dropping me off for my first day of school, feeling completely out of my comfort zone. There was a sense of awkwardness in the air as neither party really knew what to expect from the other. Despite Rob being an incredibly sweet man, the same fear that filled my mind as we initially made our way upstairs suddenly came flooding back. To be fair, I'm not sure Rob was expecting to have three Aussies dumped on him that morning, but much like every other member of the crew he couldn't have been more inviting.

'So, do you watch the new episodes?' Rob asked. Not wanting to lie, I replied with 'Honestly, not every episode, but the ones I've seen like "Barthood" are fantastic.' I wasn't quite sure what I'd said, but the ear-to-ear smile on Rob's face meant I'd certainly passed the test. Little did I know at the time, Rob directed 'Barthood', so with that stamp of approval we were off to the races.

For the next two hours, we were offered one of the most incredible insights into the making of an episode that I could ever hope to experience. It was so pleasing to see that for a man who has been working on the show for over 20 years, Rob is still just as big of a fan as the rest of us. You could feel his passion as he explained the purpose and meaning of sight gags that literally appear onscreen for no more than a second, or the painstaking process of animating scenes such as Bart running down a flight of stairs. It truly made me appreciate the show's animation on a whole new level as I realised just how much these animators continue to push themselves to achieve what would be impossible for the rest of us.

Then came the highlight of the whole day – getting to draw the characters. I'd spent countless hours as a child practising my Homer, so of course Rob asked me to draw Marge. I panicked a little because I'd never really attempted Marge before, however I wasn't going to let this opportunity slip. It was in this moment that I was sitting in Rob's chair drawing Marge Simpson with his stylus that I became a little overwhelmed with the whole scenario. Nicola has since told me that I was apparently grinning the entire time. For someone who'd never used a stylus before I was rather proud of my efforts, despite how bad it looked once compared to Rob's. On that note, an interesting observation he made was that he's able to recognise which animator has worked on an episode purely by the way they draw Marge's hair. 'It should always have a nice curve to it.'

By the time Nikki arrived to pick us up 'from school' it was time for lunch. Standing in line at the downstairs café, the vast options of sushi distracted me from realising that the man in front of me was the incredible David Silverman. Then to my left I saw Mike B. Anderson, director of classics such as 'Homer's Phobia' and 'You Only Move Twice'. Learning that even Mike knew of our podcast is something I'll never forget.

Up next was a trip to the colouring department, where Eli Balser showed me some of the most incredible animation cels I've ever seen. Holding these cels from some of my favourite episodes can only be compared to the feeling of holding someone else's newborn child, for these weren't just Scratchy's arm, these were fully fleshed out classic scenes from the 90s. I was literally holding a piece of the episode. I couldn't believe it. My personal favourites were the cels of 'The Thing & I' from 'Treehouse of Horror VII', featuring Hugo and the pigeon-rat.

The visit then came to an all-too-abrupt end with an obligatory group photo in front of the Simpson family mural in the studio's kitchen area. Looking back, if there's one thing that this experience taught me it's that the staff who work at *The Simpsons* are some of the nicest, most genuine people you will ever meet. To them, I was literally a stranger off the street, but that didn't stop them from putting their work aside for a few minutes to give me a memory that would last a lifetime.

Season 5 (1993-94)
In Conversation

DANDO: While Season 4 dipped its toe into a new brand of comedy, Season 5 dove straight into the deep end. The first five episodes are instant classics that feature heavily on fans' 'Top Ten' lists, especially 'Homer Goes to College' and 'Cape Feare'.

MITCH: Not to mention 'Rosebud', an episode so good it made me want to go out and watch *Citizen Kane*. Both undoubtedly classics, but if I had to pull one off the shelf to watch again on a Sunday afternoon, I'd be reaching for the one starring C. M. Burns every day of the week. It's such a pure tale about a man and his bear, and made me feel a lot better about still taking a teddy to school up until a frighteningly late age in life.

D: How late?

M: Graduation.

D: Well, as an avid Beatles fan, I've always had a soft spot for 'Homer's Barbershop Quartet'. You can tell the writers and animators were all Beatles fans themselves since they managed to work in a plethora of references to the Fab Four that any fan can appreciate.

M: Or, at the very least, they clearly did a lot of research of archival footage.

D: Exactly. From the infamous 'Let It Be' sessions photo recreation, to Barney wanting to take contemporary music to strange new places with his track 'Number 8', the staff treat the band and their history with a lot of respect.

M: After that massive start to Season 5, there's a forgotten gem in 'Marge on the Lam'. I think this is an episode that was easy to gloss over as a young boy, as were most Marge-centric episodes, but it's one I'd highly recommend going back to watch again. It's a brilliant parody of *Thelma and Louise*, and has more moments of brilliant comedy than most people would remember. It also taught me that good waffles stick together, and how to cook engine-block eggs.

D: Although it stars the amazing Al Brooks, 'Bart's Inner Child' is probably the weakest link of the season. Brooks' talents feel wasted on Brad Goodman and the story doesn't really appear to know its end goal. It does however feature one of my favourite Smithers and Burns conversations where Smithers confesses his love for his boss, only to take it back immediately.

M: Goodman is the only Brooks character who doesn't have any memorable quotes. I think by writing such a calm, placid character, it robbed Brooks of his natural hyper-energy that so many of his characters are filled with. Interestingly, whilst Goodman's character was modelled on motivational speaker John Bradshaw, he appears to be physically modelled on Brooks himself. It was almost like the animators wanted to gift him that much to say thanks for what was already a great catalogue of guest characters.

D: Until now Bart had been the face of the show. However, with the writers now pushing the boundaries further than ever before, it became clear that there was so much more they could do with an adult than a 10-year-old child. Do you think this was when Homer started to become the primary focus?

M: I think he always had a share of episodes where he was a central character, but it started to change from events happening around him to things happening *to* him. So, rather than Homer having to work harder because Lisa is getting a pony, it's the family having to react to Homer going into space. That said, there's a block in the middle of Season 4 that was also strongly focused on Homer.

D: What can't be argued is that it's Bart and Homer who are the front-runners. Almost two thirds of the episodes are based around the two, with Marge and Lisa only getting one episode each dedicated to them: 'Marge on the Lam' and 'Lisa vs. Malibu Stacy'.

M: You could make a case for '$pringfield' revolving around Marge's gambling addiction at a push, but there was certainly an imbalance. Particularly with Marge, it seems that the writers get stuck on variations on the same theme: Marge, bored with home life, tries to break out. I guess there's only so many ways you can tell that story.

D: 'Homer Goes to College' and the wraparounds in 'Tree-house of Horror IV' were Conan O'Brien's final contributions to the show. Although he went on to achieve huge success in late-night television, as a *Simpsons* fan you can only imagine what gems we'd been treated to had he stayed on as a writer. Homer is written to perfection in 'Homer Goes to College', an episode where there's never a dull moment. Homer yelling 'Nerrrrddd!' out of the car window is always the highlight for me.

M: He's written with the perfect mix of knowledge and ignorance. By that I mean he clearly has a *lot* of knowledge of college movies, and how you are supposed to act should you find yourself in one. However, he is completely ignorant of the fact that *nobody* aside from himself is acting that way. He so badly wants the Dean to be crusty and old that he's completely blind to him being young and open-minded.

D: I love the way this season sees Homer thrown into unique situations with characters we'd only even seen him share a few scenes with, like his trek with Apu to meet the head of the Kwik-E-Mart in 'Homer and Apu' . . .

M: Of all the visual jokes that *The Simpsons* has ever created, I feel like this episode has some of its very best. Homer and Apu trekking on donkeys, only for it to be revealed they are yet to leave Springfield, or the world's first ever convenience store perched atop the Indian Alps feel like jokes straight out of *The Naked Gun* to me.

D: Or his classic jury duty stint with Principal Skinner in 'The Boy Who Knew Too Much'. Skinner is the perfect foil to Homer's shenanigans, with Homer being too excited by the prospect of watching *Free Willy* to worry about ensuring justice is served.

M: To be fair, Skinner is the perfect foil to just about any character on the show. Skinner is essentially an inactive volcano. Placid on the surface, but quietly bubbling away underneath, only very occasionally showing glimpses of his rage. Here though, we mostly just see him as a symbol of repression. Even his attempt to connect with Homer via a TV reference is met with a swift 'Shut up!'

D: Homer's relationship with Flanders is also explored in 'Homer Loves Flanders', an episode that has one of the more underrated heartfelt moments in the series when Homer defends Flanders in church.

M: That whole episode is hugely important in kind of resetting how we see Flanders as an audience member. He really is desperate to see the good in all fellow humans, and it says a lot that only Homer could possibly corrupt him, to the point that he even lies in front of his children. Rather than coming across as an occasionally smarmy has-it-better-than-you-and-quietly-revels-in-it character, we see Ned as a man who desperately believes in, and loves, his community. So, when that community is inadvertently turned against him by Homer, but it's Homer that comes to his rescue, it really is a gut-punch moment.

D: Shearer's delivery of Flanders' 'thank-you' is so perfect that you feel like he had to have been on the verge of tears when recording.

M: Season 5 continued along the trend started in Season 4 of including several high-concept episodes. While there was still plenty of time for a small number like 'Secrets of a Successful Marriage', the show was starting to gradually set us up for the future where nothing from *X-Files* tie-ins to murderous robots were off limits.

D: Well, it was quite bold for the show to send Homer into space. That was certainly a concept that would never have even been considered in the earlier years, yet the writers managed to deliver a believable, family-driven story that allowed Castellaneta to showcase his full range.

M: 'Deep Space Homer' almost feels like watching a Jim Carrey comedy from the mid-90s where directors would essentially just point a camera at him and say 'go'. It's a tour de force by Dan, but what I really think helps seal the episode is the inanimate carbon rod, who I think was robbed for the Emmy for Best Supporting Actor that year.

D: One of my favourite guest spots in the whole season is Conan O'Brien in 'Bart Gets Famous', which was actually recorded before he had even begun hosting *Late Night*. Bringing Conan back was a nice gesture from his former colleagues, and a sign of respect for his many contributions to the show.

M: And a sign of belief and confidence in the fact that he was destined for bigger things. I mean, I'd be too terrified to record that dialogue in case I jinxed myself. Of course, I am not Conan O'Brien.

'The Last Temptation of Homer'
(Season 5, Episode 9)
Review by Dando

When Homer finds himself attracted to a beautiful new co-worker named Mindy, he does everything he can to avoid her, only to be sent to a power expo in Capital City with her for work. Back in Springfield, Bart is diagnosed with poor vision, a dry scalp, and sunken arches, with the resulting corrective items rendering him a nerd. In Capital City, Homer is torn between loyalty and temptation.

Adultery is an issue that *The Simpsons* has never been afraid of tackling. In fact, it was only the eighth episode when we saw Marge almost do the unthinkable and cheat on Homer with the smooth-talking bowling instructor, Jacques. It's a pretty heavy subject for a show that's targeted at children as much as it is adults, yet 'The Last Temptation of Homer' manages to provide entertainment on both ends of the comedy spectrum with a story that I've appreciated far more, the older I get. While the kids are laughing at how funny Barney looks dressed in a bikini while singing the 'I Dream of Jeannie' theme, adults are laughing at the awkwardness of Homer and Mindy discussing 'getting off together' in an elevator.

This isn't the first time Homer has found himself in a situation that could destroy his marriage, the difference being that in 'Colonel Homer' the feelings weren't mutual. Homer is completely innocent in that situation as he remains oblivious to Lurleen's advances, quickly rushing back to Marge's side once the reality of the moment sinks in. Marge is Homer's safety net, she's the one woman who understands him and remains loyal through the bad times, and it's because of this that I've always had an issue with Homer kissing Mindy in this episode's final scene. It's only a peck, I get that, but I for one know that I'd be furious if I found out my wife kissed another man in such a way on a business trip. All that aside, at least Homer makes the correct decision in the end, resolving the issue by replacing Mindy with the love of his life.

I can't think of any other time when Homer is so consistently mature. As confused as he is by these new feelings, hilariously blaming the powdered gravy he ate in the parking lot, he still does all he can to control them even though everything in his life seems to be telling him to do otherwise. In an ironic twist on *It's A Wonderful Life*, Homer's guardian angel proves life would have been much better had he married Mindy, ringworm commercials tell him to 'just do it'; even fortune cookies reveal that he'll find happiness with a new love. I love that of all things it's the cookie that convinces Homer that adultery is inevitable. Michelle Pfeiffer shines in that moment of truth – her delivery of 'desserts aren't always right' is perfectly earnest, showing a sense of understanding for Homer's concern mixed with disappointment that the night may not end how she'd hoped.

Pfeiffer is outstanding in her first voice acting role. It was important for Mindy to not be flirtatious but simply desirable, so that we as viewers could invest ourselves in this being a story about two decent people trying to fight unwanted urges, as opposed to a sleazebag husband screwing around with a homewrecker. Although Mindy is completely open to the idea of sleeping with Homer after their romantic dinner in Capital City, knowing full well it would ruin his marriage, she at least allows him to make the decision himself without being too forward. It's simply a moment of weakness for this overall nice woman.

To put it simply, Mindy is without question the everyman's dream. She's the type of girl you can imagine spending her Saturday afternoons drinking beer while playing video games in her underwear. The character is so genuine that it allows you to immerse yourself in Homer's situation as the temptations grow ever stronger the more time he spends with her. My favourite piece of animation in the whole episode is Homer's nervous pause before he approaches Mindy in the lunch room. He so desperately wants to prove that this infatuation is merely physical, yet there's always the chance that it could only intensify matters further.

So much of this episode is fixated on Homer and Mindy's relationship that it can be easy to forget about the side story involving Bart's plummet down the social ladder. For me there was so much more the writers could have explored here that could have quite easily been an episode in itself. Bart is only a menace on the surface, so it would have been nice to see him spend more time in the refuge of the damned and learn to embrace his new self; after all, these nerds saved him from what was surely going to be another hefty beating from the bullies.

It's a credit to the writing staff that the episode manages to incorporate a variety of wackiness into such a serious theme. For example Charlie gets sent away in a tube, Homer slides down the side of the power plant, we even get introduced to Joey Jo-Jo Junior Shabadoo, Stewart the Duck and the man with the giant hand. Most importantly, the greatest moment of them all, Mr. Burns and his 'flying' monkeys, is a movie parody that only *The Simpsons* is truly capable of.

If you've ever been in a committed relationship then 'The Last Temptation of Homer' is probably an episode you can relate to quite easily. That's not to say we've all considered leaving our partners for an attractive, donut-eating work colleague, but it's a simple ethical dilemma that we can all envision ourselves in. Homer and Mindy teach us that having feelings for others isn't the issue: it's how we act upon them that matters most.

What did we learn?

The Burmese Melon Fly has over 1,000 sex partners and suffers virtually no guilt.

'$pringfield (Or, How I Learned to Stop Worrying and Love Legalized Gambling)'
(Season 5, Episode 10)
Review by Mitch

Looking for ways to fix a declining economy, the citizens of Springfield elect to legalise gambling. Homer finds work as a blackjack dealer in Mr. Burns' casino, while Bart starts up a treehouse casino of his own. Marge, meanwhile, falls into the traps of compulsive gambling and forgets about Lisa's school pageant. While overlooking the whole affair, Mr. Burns slowly descends into madness.

When I first started telling family and friends about this book, I was surprised at just how many people were excited to read it. I don't think it had anything to do with me, whatsoever, just that so many people were truly excited to get back into the show. That said, as surprised as I was by those positive reactions, I was absolutely blown away when a colleague told me they'd never seen an episode, and asked me to recommend where to start . . . 'An evaluation of your childhood' was my shocked reply.

It did get me thinking, though. If you had to show somebody an episode of *The Simpsons* that encapsulates all that the show has to offer, what would it be? It's a show that can be so many things to so many people, loved by all for varied but valid reasons. As I thought about many of my favourites, there was one I kept coming back to . . . the crazy tale of Mr. Burns building a casino, and Marge's ensuing gambling addiction.

It's one of the few occasions where each main character in the family has their own compelling plot. Not only that, every character is taken out of their comfort zone but all remain true to who they are. It almost holds up as a mini-movie plot rather than a TV episode, and would have made a great script to stretch out to 90 minutes. We get a look at a more prosperous Springfield in an opening flashback. Unfortunately, the floating car industry didn't hold up in the long run, and a city with streets paved with gold soon found itself run-down and struggling. Despite having lived in this city for four and a half seasons now, this is the first time we get to see a real attempt to tell a story about its character.

The decision to turn to legalised gambling is a realistic one, which keeps the plot, if not the comedy, grounded in reality. At the town hall meeting, there is an important moment when the whole town expects Marge to complain, but surprisingly she agrees that a casino could be a good idea. Ironic, given that she experiences the worst of what gambling has to offer later in the episode. The town hall also revels in a favourite pastime of the show: poking fun at mob mentality. Even a burp is enough to solicit cheers from the town as they all race out of the meeting, and straight into a cesspool of sex and drugs.

One thing *The Simpsons* has always done is show the

perils of vice. Homer may drink a lot, but Moe's and its inhabitants are never seen in a positive light. This moral view is no different here, as we see Marge become hooked by poker machines after turning a lost quarter into a dollar. The show could arguably have gone further as we don't ever see the financial ramification of her actions, but we do see an emotional one. As a direct result of Marge's gambling, Maggie is nearly eaten by a tiger, Lisa is forced to go to a pageant as a monster version of 'Floreda', and Homer and the kids nearly fall victim to the boogeyman! Truly, when 'Gamblor' has sunk his neon claws into you, there is no escape.

I firmly believe that the best episodes have some emotional weight behind the comedy, so this episode has one of my favourite endings. Julie Kavner's quiet delivery as she admits she has an addiction is one of the only 'real' moments of the episode, but it was a brilliant choice to end things on that note. It brings to a close a brilliant episode that really should appear in more top-10 lists than it does.

And what of that colleague of mine? Last I saw him, he was holding up a scale replica of a Ferrari, insisting that his wife 'hop in'. I'll consider that a successful *Simpsons* conversion.

What did we learn?

Robert Goulet will play anywhere.

'Cape Feare'
(Season 5, Episode 2)
In Conversation

After being released on parole, Sideshow Bob attempts to murder Bart. The family enter the witness protection programme and relocate to Terror Lake, but wherever they run, Bob is waiting.

DANDO: This episode is monumental in that although it aired during Season 5, it was a holdover from Season 4, making it the final episode produced by the original writing team. Whether by design or coincidence, I can't think of a better episode to send off one of television's greatest creative ensembles.

MITCH: With that information, it feels like they threw in *every* idea they had left in the tank. The first thing I noticed when I went back to watch *Cape Feare* was how much exists that I'd forgotten about. I don't think I'd be the only person who didn't remember that this is where *Up Late with McBain* came from, for example.

D: I'd also completely forgotten about some of the non-Bob-related scenes, such as our first insight into Moe's double life as an animal smuggler. It's so unexpected that it catches me off guard every single time.

M: Normally for an episode that's so loved, people would remember every second, but I think what happens here is, the towering performance of Kelsey as Sideshow Bob

163

makes you forget about almost anything else in this episode.

D: The best thing about those sorts of memory lapses is that they let you get a big laugh out of Moe's panda smuggling operation every single time.

M: Amazingly, the high rate of jokes in the first act only speeds up once Bob is let out of prison and starts his quest for revenge.

D: It's interesting how long it took for Bob to be revealed as the person behind the threatening letters to Bart. I'd like to know whether it came as a surprise to many viewers when it first aired or whether Grammer's appearance was heavily advertised in the lead-up.

M: You have to remember that prior to this episode Bob had never attacked Bart, so this truly was the birth of one of the series' longest-running story arcs.

D: Looking back now it's so obvious that Bob is the culprit since we have all grown accustomed to his desire to kill Bart.

M: And the musical score is a giveaway as it has since become Bob's theme.

D: I genuinely feel sorry for Bart as he deals with the pressures of receiving death threats in the mail. This would be terrifying for the best of us, let alone a child, yet nobody besides Marge seems to be taking the situation seriously. Homer, as always, is totally oblivious.

M: My personal highlight of the episode is Homer's ability to out-obnoxious Bob in the theatre, smoking a bigger cigar and laughing more disruptively than Bob ever could.

D: Or being completely unaware that bursting into Bart's bedroom with a chainsaw and hockey mask may be a little confronting given the circumstances, especially since it comes just moments after entering the room while brandishing a butcher's knife.

M: As you said, this is a horrible situation for Bart, but the jokes come so fast there's very little time to dwell on it. Just to rattle off a few of the iconic moments from this episode, we've got the cactus patch, 'Hello, Mr. Thompson', and of course, the rakes.

D: What's amazing about the rakes is that one of the series' most iconic moments was born out of pure necessity. Originally Bob was only going to step on one rake and be done with it, but with the episode falling well short of the required run time the decision was made to extend it out into a moment so fitting for a character as dignified as Bob. Despite his unmistakable intelligence and attention to detail, Bob manages to fall victim to the easiest of foils, in this case, garden utensils. Why are there so many rakes on the ground?

M: Who cares! I would love to have seen Kelsey's first reaction to watching the rake scene, given that he only recorded the grumble once and, like Bob, wouldn't have seen this coming.

D: I hope he loved it! It's a great visual that pays homage to classic Warner Bros. cartoons. In fact, the writers compare Bob's hunt for Bart to that of Wile E. Coyote's quest for capturing the Road Runner, which was the inspiration for Bob's head being trampled by a parade of elephants.

M: The thing is, Bob is such a contradictory character in that he has this genius-level intellect, but often misses the forest for the trees and falls victim to the simplest of pratfalls. A snapshot of that is on display when he is writing menacing letters in blood, and follows it up by a to-do list, and a letter to 'These United States'.

D: Even Snake is smart enough to know that's not a good idea!

M: *The Simpsons* has included a lot of great movie parodies over the years, but some of the work in parodying *Cape Fear* is out of this world. It includes the obvious references – the tattoos, exiting prison, the palm-trees shirt – but it also goes to extra lengths that only true cinephiles would appreciate. They use camera techniques never seen on the show before that brilliantly mimic Scorsese's camera direction in the 1991 film. There are so many slow twisting zooms that make the camera become a character in itself, and that gives the episode a feeling of menace unlike any other. That sort of effort shows a huge love and respect for the source material.

D: The musical score is another element that intensifies the feeling in a way we'd never seen. It virtually became Bob's theme from this point on, but it's never matched the story as well as it does here.

M: There's even a 30–40 second or so moment of Bart running around on the houseboat as Bob is chasing him where there's virtually no dialogue and the music ramps up that feels like it belongs in a cinema, not on home TV.

D: The final attack is genuinely menacing . . .

M: I love the direction as the boat sails down the river as it allows the darkness of the situation to build up, which makes the payoff of Bob singing the score to the *HMS Pinafore* so much better, not to mention unexpected.

D: I would give anything to see footage of Kelsey performing this in the recording studio. It's still probably the best version of 'He is an Englishman' that I've ever heard.

166

M: In true *Simpsons* style, the police are shown to be completely useless yet again. Chief Wiggum's dimwittedness is on full display, not getting the joke 'Chief Piggum'. Of course, later he needs to be corrected about there being a law against writing threatening letters. Even the fact that Bob gets caught at all is because Wiggum, Lou and Ed are . . . let's say, 'raiding' a brothel. In bathrobes.

D: As a kid, it always baffled me why the police were wearing their bathrobes when they arrested Bob. The only explanation I could think of was that they must've raced out of bed with no time to get dressed.

M: Sweet, innocent Dando.

D: The only negative is that for an episode so iconic, the ending is pretty weak.

M: Yeah, ending this brilliant cinematic story on a non sequitur about Grampa becoming a woman is a little baffling.

D: Granted, it's hard to follow a sequence that includes Kelsey Grammer's stirring rendition of *HMS Pinafore*, but why follow it at all?

M: I suppose they wanted to include a scene of the family returning to Springfield and needed a joke in that moment, but it just took me a little out of the episode, rather than let me soak in the epic musical finale.

D: Still, it's a small price to pay for one of the greatest episodes of all time.

What did we learn?

Once a man is in your home, anything you do to him is nice and legal.

A Tribute to 'Treehouse of Horror'

Dando

As a child, I'd spend countless hours at the local video store just browsing through the different covers of the horror section, trying to imagine what would happen in the films. I had to imagine because the owner Pete knew my parents and there was no way he was ever going to let me hire *A Nightmare on Elm Street* at the age of six. That is why the 'Treehouse of Horror' series meant so much to me growing up. It was a way of getting a sneak peek into these movies I'd heard so much about like *The Shining* and *Child's Play*, like a backstage pass that my mum didn't know about.

Unfortunately for all Australian fans growing up in the 90s. Halloween was never really celebrated, in fact it's only now just starting to pick up steam, in the last two or three years. For some reason, I'd always wanted to go trick-or-treating dressed as Lard Lad, even having my costume ready to go: orange wig from the $2 shop, blue overalls and the giant inflatable donut from the pool in our backyard. Had the cosplaying industry been as popular then as it is now, you can only imagine how many Devil Flanders and pigeon-rats there'd have been floating around the convention circuit.

'Treehouse of Horror' episodes are almost like porn for

horror and sci-fi buffs. With the freedom of being non-canon, the writers and animators are able to sneak in an abundance of references and parodies that showcase their love for the genre. My personal favourite is the gremlin sabotaging the school bus in 'Terror at 5½ Feet', a parody of The Twilight Zone's 'Nightmare at 20,000 Feet'. It's hard to look past the genius of 'The Shinning' though; for me it seems *that's* the one everybody remembers so fondly. So much so that it's not uncommon for fans to accidentally refer to the Stanley Kubrick classic by its *Simpsons* counterpart.

Homer[3] is the one segment that will always have a place in my heart, as it takes me back to when my Mum's '*Simpsons* ban' finally came to an end. 'Treehouse of Horror VI' was the first new Halloween Special to air once said ban was lifted and I remember being so excited because all week Channel 10 were hyping it as 'for the first time see The Simpsons in 3D!' That segment was so ground-breaking for its time and is a perfect example of the talent of the *Simpsons* animation department.

Now despite them being an absolute joy to watch as a fan, the 'Treehouse of Horror' episodes are also incredibly time-consuming for the staff. Knowing this makes me appreciate them even more as it shows just how much the writers and animators must love producing them. You can only imagine how stressful it must be for the writers having to think of a way to cram three stories into 22 minutes, while the animators have to essentially redesign so many of the show's characters and backgrounds. I remember hearing during a DVD commentary that Jean and Reiss almost scrapped the concept because of how difficult it was becoming. Thankfully they didn't, as this annual tradition is one of the last remaining pieces we have left from the show's earlier years.

Dando's Top 10 'Treehouse of Horror' Segments

1. 'Nightmare Cafeteria'
2. 'Terror at 5½ Feet'
3. 'Homer³'
4. 'The Shinning'
5. 'Nightmare on Evergreen Terrace'
6. 'The HΩmega Man'
7. 'Time and Punishment'
8. 'Clown Without Pity'
9. 'The Devil and Homer Simpson'
10. 'The Thing and I'

Mitch

While Australia might not have celebrated Halloween when I was growing up, there's one common tradition that we did share, and that was telling ghost stories to your friends. Telling stories around a campfire, or table, or anywhere else that a few of your friends have gathered, is a rite of passage that teaches us much about humanity. We learn our friends' deepest fears, and they learn ours. There's a weird kind of primal joy in fear, so when watching that original 'Treehouse of Horror' (the only one that actually took place in the treehouse), despite never having experienced Halloween, I found it really easy to relate to Bart and Lisa.

As the years went on, TOH became an annual tradition to be looked forward to. The sandbox environment
created a sense of anticipation that couldn't be matched
by regular episodes, as the sense of danger where anything could happen to any character only existed within
these mini-trilogies. It was a world where Homer could
shoot Flanders, or be turned into a jack-in-the-box at a
moment's notice. No matter what, you were guaranteed
to see something you hadn't seen before.

Like Dando, I found these episodes provided a window
into a world of horror and sci-fi that I hadn't seen before.
The very first TOH introduced me to *The Amityville
Horror, The Twilight Zone* and Edgar Allan Poe. Without
even realising it, I was being given a first-class course in
classic horror, sci-fi and literature. I admit, it was a bit of
a stretch when I put that down on my résumé under 'Further education', but it genuinely did make me feel smarter.
I could quote Poe at age five without ever having picked up
one of his books. By seven I could tell you about the tragedy of *King Kong* despite never having seen the film.

The benefit of a non-canon setting, combined with a
heavy dose of references to other films and TV shows, is
that the TOH series has aged brilliantly. When I first
watched Francis Ford Coppola's *Dracula*, I enjoyed
thinking back to the amazing visual parody of Burns'
spectre overlooking the family's passage to the castle
more than I enjoyed the movie itself. Admittedly, that
may have had something to do with Keanu Reeves'
accent in the film. Similarly, when I first read Ray Brad-
bury's 'A Sound of Thunder' I did so picturing Homer as
the story's protagonist.

The 'Treehouse of Horror' segment is still one of the

most relevant episodes to me. I don't get to watch new episodes of *The Simpsons* each week any more, but I do make sure I track down each TOH segment. That feeling of relevance seems to translate into the wider community, as the news that Sideshow Bob would kill Bart Simpson in TOH 26 spread like wildfire on the internet. The switch to digital has given the animators greater ability to alter the look of the episodes to remain faithful to their source material as well – as recently seen in that same episode's picturesque black & white reimagining of *Godzilla*.

Like birthdays, TOH is an annual joy for me where I'm guaranteed to like at least two of my three gifts. Long may its tradition live on. Without further ado, here are my Top 10 segments. (Dando actually stole my thunder on a couple, such as 'The Shinning' and 'Nightmare on Evergreen Terrace', so I've swapped them out to avoid double-up. That's just the kind of guy I am.)

Mitch's Top 10 'Treehouse of Horror' *Segments*

1. 'The Raven'
2. 'Attack of the 50-Foot Eyesores'
3. 'The Genesis Tub'
4. 'Fly vs. Fly'
5. 'The Bart Zone'
6. 'Bart Simpson's Dracula'
7. 'Citizen Kang'
8. 'Dial 'Z' for Zombies'
9. 'Hungry are the Damned'
10. 'Desperately Xeeking Xena'

Four Finger Discount's 'Treehouse of Horror'

Now, a while ago Dando and I thought that if we were to sit here and critique other people's work, we really should try our hand at putting up some of our own. Given our joy for 'Treehouse of Horror', it seemed like the perfect vehicle for three story pitches that we could play around in with total freedom.

We sent the following ideas to Al Jean and were thrilled when he took the time to reply to us. We were, sadly, less excited when his reply informed us that current policy forbids him from reading scripts sent in by freelancers.

Regardless, there's nothing that says we can't share it with you, dear reader.

We hope you enjoy . . .

Act One: GROANING LISA

A zombie plague is slowly starting to spread around Springfield. We are in the very, very early stages, with nobody knowing what's happening and several references to people not turning up to work/school, etc. Miss Hoover is amongst the people who haven't turned up to

175

work. This is especially annoying for Lisa, who was really looking forward to handing in an assignment early for extra credit. Not willing to miss out on a potential A++, she heads to Miss Hoover's house on the way home. She finds the front door unlocked and goes inside, intending to drop her work off for her to read, but as she is doing so, a zombie Miss Hoover lunges at Lisa and bites her. Understandably freaked out, Lisa races home where she almost immediately starts to feel unwell, passing out instantly after making it to her room.

By the following morning, news of the outbreak has spread. Miss Hoover is identified as patient zero, and Marge, knowing Lisa was going to see her, fears the worst. She checks on her room to find that Lisa has turned. Zombie Lisa, about to attack Marge, is distracted by seeing Homer trying to figure out 'Professor Provolones Picto-Puzzle', referring back to 'Lisa the Simpson'. She studies the puzzle, seemingly stuck to the spot, allowing the family to think they are safe, until she solves it in about three seconds. Homer, Marge and Bart rush out of the house with Maggie to discover most of the town have turned, apart from Dr. Nick who is trying to find a cure. When they find him, he's running an *I Am Legend*-style series of trials on a group of infected residents, greeting them with a hearty 'Hi, every zombie!' as he injects them with various condiments and ointments, trying to find a cure.

Marge lures Lisa to his trial room, where Homer, leaving a door unlocked, causes the zombies to escape and kill Dr. Nick.

The pack bears down on the Simpson family, but at

the last second Lisa recognises them and groans out a communication to stop the attack. Having realised that the zombies can be controlled to some extent, the surviving inhabitants of Springfield try to adjust to life with the zombies, even finding that productivity at the power plant has increased. Lisa becomes an advocate for zombie rights, and we close on a Zombie Rights debate between Lisa and Donald Trump. Lisa makes a slurring and groaning speech with no distinguishable words, which is met by a round of supportive groans and applause from zombies in the audience. Donald Trump gives a rebuttal, but speaks in the same guttural groaning, and is met by the same groaning by his human supporters in the audience.

Act Two: JURASSIC PORK

At the power plant, the daily donut delivery is noticed to have contained an expensive jelly-filled donut amongst the usual selection. As it turns out, the donuts were intended for Rainier Wolfcastle, filming an adaptation of *Billy and the Cloneasaurus* nearby. Under threat of litigation from the movie studio if the donuts aren't returned, Smithers places the delivery under lock and key in the lunch room, to be sent back the following day. Homer hatches a plan to smuggle the rare jelly-filled donut home from the lunch room. He starts by switching off the plant's security systems by sneaking into Smithers' office. Using a temperature-controlled container disguised as a mailing tube, he loads the donuts up and races home, leaving Smithers staring at a computer monitor featuring a topless Mr. Burns repeating 'ah-ah-ah' as he tries to restart the system.

Driving home victorious, Homer starts devouring his bounty. While he is lost in the moment he doesn't realise that the strawberry-filled donut rolls out of the tube and slips behind the brake pedal. Attempting to slow down as he nears his home, he squashes the donut, causing filling to squirt into his eye, temporarily blinding him and causing him to run over and kill Plopper, AKA Spider Pig. Distraught, Homer takes his body into town to 'Give him a proper goodbye'. He returns with a leg of ham, several pork chops, and countless rashers of bacon, all arranged delicately on a platter with a bereavement card from a funeral home.

He mournfully eats all but one slice of bacon, which he keeps as a memento. He heads to Moe's after his final meal to drink away his sorrows. When he tells Moe of this last piece of bacon, a mad scientist (special guest star, Jeff Goldblum) overhears and offers Homer his services. From the final rasher of bacon, Plopper's DNA is extracted and he is successfully cloned. Everything goes well at first, until Plopper defies all natural law by becoming pregnant and giving birth to three piglets. The piglets immediately display acts of aggression towards the family, along with super-intelligence, and soon start to hunt them in their own house. Bart attempts to distract the pigs by luring them to a feeding tray, only to see one of the pigs working on a plan to lure Homer to a feeding tray of their own. When Bart sees Homer falling for it, he delivers the immortal line 'Clever girl'.

In the climactic showdown, the three piglets have Maggie cornered and rush for her. Homer runs in from the side, throwing up his hands à la Chris Pratt in *Jurassic World* to try and stop the pigs attacking, only to have them all jump on him and overpower him. Their tiny, cute, relentless hooves beat him to a pulp, before Plopper sacrifices himself to save Homer. He fights the three piglets, but is outmatched. They kill him but, unluckily for them, he collapses on top of them, rendering the fight a tragic draw.

Homer, keen to make sure that nothing like this ever happens again, sets about disposing of the pigs the only way he knows how, and John Williams' theme from *Jurassic Park* slowly swells around Homer devouring pork chop after pork chop. In the final scene, Homer, feeling the after-effects of having eaten four pigs in one sitting, lies on the couch in pain.

'What's wrong with him?' asks Marge.

Goldblum's scientist replies, 'He was so caught up with whether or not he could, he didn't stop to think if he should.'

Act Three: ONE FOR THE BELCHERS

For the finale, we have a direct reference to the second ever episode of *The Twilight Zone*, 'One for the Angels'. In it, Death comes for a salesman, who manages to trick Death into not taking him. Having to fill a quota, Death decides to take a young girl in the building instead. Overcome with guilt, the man pitches to Death to take him instead, finally delivering his pitch for the angels, saving the little girl by giving up his own life. This final segment is also a parody of *The Truman Show*, where the Simpsons discover that they are only actors in a television show, after discovering a commercial about themselves . . .

Homer is watching TV during an electrical storm, despite Marge's protestation that it's too dangerous to be using electrical goods. He assures her that he installed a new circuit breaker. When she asks if he means 'installed' or merely 'bought' a look of panic comes over his face. He rushes to the kitchen to grab it, but in that time a huge lightning bolt strikes the house, killing the TV instantly, leaving an eerie glow coming from the antenna.

The following day he purchases a new TV, and soon discovers a wide range of shows he has never heard of before. Lisa works out that the lightning must have changed the frequency of the antenna. As Homer channel-surfs, he sees a bunch of commercials for TV shows we are all familiar with, prompting him to ask 'Conan O'Brien. I thought he got fired?'

Then comes the moment that stops the family in its tracks: a promo for the last ever episode of *The Simpsons*. The promo highlights some of the touchstone moments from their history, and it dawns on them that their lives have all been a set-up, with an array of radio-jammers blocking out any news from the real world that would interfere with their timeline.

The Simpson family break the news to the townspeople, the majority of whom had no idea their lives were a sham. The only person who knew the truth was Burns, who had to power the network's massive broadcasting vans.

Everyone in the town fears for the future if the show is to be cancelled and call a meeting to decide on a course of action. The whole cast descends upon FOX HQ, where they send Grampa Simpson in as a delegate to pitch the continuation of the show to Rupert Murdoch who, they find, was solely responsible for the decision. Grampa calls upon all the truly great moments of the show and reminds everybody about what has made the show so loved.

Rupert is so moved by Grampa Simpson that he agrees to keep the show on the air – but at a price. In order to fit within budget constraints, he will have to cancel *Bob's Burgers*. This is even worse news to Homer, as *Bob's Burgers* has been a favourite show of his ever since he was able to pick up new channels. As they walk down the FOX hallways, they see Bob Belcher clearing out his office, packing a lone Emmy into a box. Homer pleads with everybody to reconsider. His plea falls on deaf ears, as everybody is desperate to just get back to how things were, but on the way out they walk past the offices of their show and see a trophy cabinet dedicated to them, overflowing with golden awards statues, and decide they've had a good enough run.

They send Grampa back in to Rupert to plead with him to cancel the show. Rupert ponders the decision for a while, tossing a scythe back and forth between his hands as he decides who to cut. Unable to bring himself to let go of all of the love and joy he has realised the show has brought him, he is seconds away from firing the Belchers when an accountant comes in and shows him the salary figure Bart is negotiating now that he's learned he is a star. Rupert's eyes narrow and harden in an instant, all love is washed away from his face, and he unceremoniously fires the entire cast. Cut to black.

Written by 'Mutilating' Mitch Grinter and 'Bone-crushing' Brendan Dando

Season 6 (1994-95)
In Conversation

MITCH: Season 6 is almost unfairly good. By now the show has that feeling of a well-oiled machine pumping out perfection over and over again. Kind of like Roger Federer, only funny, and with displays of emotion. The evolution towards out and out comedy was complete by this point. There were still episodes that had an emotional beat, but there were plenty that didn't worry about a moral or a dilemma and just focused on telling great stories with lots of jokes.

DANDO: Is that why you don't call this your favourite season?

M: I think so . . . it's not to say that these episodes aren't great. When you are going to focus on jokes without as much substance beneath them, the comedy needs to be great and it all hits the mark here, but personally I think the earlier episodes have a little more resonance. We're talking small amounts, though. It's like trying to choose your favourite child.

D: It's funny you'd bring up the less frequent emotional beats, because this season contains what I consider the most powerful ending to any *Simpsons* episode with 'And Maggie Makes Three'. When it's revealed that Homer has kept all of his photos of Maggie where he needs the most cheering up, turning the 'Don't Forget, You're Here Forever' sign at his workstation into 'Do It

For Her'. To me it's about as perfect as *The Simpsons* can be.

M: Don't get me wrong, they could definitely still turn it on when they wanted to, but whereas in the past it was interwoven in all episodes, now for every 'And Maggie Makes Three' there was a 'Homie the Clown'.

D: Another ending that never fails to pull at the heartstrings is that of 'Lisa On Ice'. With a younger sister of my own, I can't help but get goosebumps during the closing moments of the hockey final as Bart and Lisa reminisce about the times they've both been there for each other. I've always had a close relationship with my sister and this moment will always remind me of all of the good times we've been lucky enough to share together.

M: True story: I used to have a Roger Rabbit toy that was remarkably similar to Mr. Hunny Bunny. Around the time of this episode going to air, my dog had chewed it beyond recognition. I remember feeling a great level of empathy for Bart when he haplessly tried to put him back together.

D: It also gifts anybody who has ever played social or competitive sport so much to relate to.

M: I know many men who, despite being well into their thirties, still insist that they only get to ride in the front because they're a good guy at sports. I also love the reckless abandon with which Apu discover's Lisa's talent, firing a hockey puck for her to stop with her bare hands.

D: This season provided us with the first flash-forward episode in 'Lisa's Wedding', a nice change from the several flashbacks we'd already seen in previous seasons.

M: It's always nice to see what might happen in the future, as there's that lure of the unknown. Using a fortune teller as a device to be able to tell their story but then return to the enclosed time-loop of Springfield was a clever touch.

D: It's a little strange going back and watching it now since the supposed future they speak of is 2010; however, for me that only adds to the charm. The writers were bold in their predictions of how the world would look 15 years in the future.

M: Unfortunately, like most bold visions, reality falls behind. I'm yet to see a school sponsored by Pepsi, for example. That said, on a happier front, we're yet to have lived through World War III.

D: Personally, I love how the first thing we see in the future are what seem like robots walking down the street, only for it be revealed that they're simply actors in costume heading to auditions for *The Wizard of Oz*.

M: As opposed to the real robots later revealed to explode after self-actualising.

D: However, the strongest aspect of the episode is the emotional roller coaster that Lisa finds herself on. Her entire life she's felt like an outsider, never really understanding where she fits into the madness that is Springfield. The story follows a similar path to that of 'Lisa's Substitute', except this time Mr. Bergstrom is replaced with a strapping young Englishman named Hugh.

M: Who I was shocked to learn was voiced by Inigo Montoya himself, Mandy Patinkin. It's amazing how often an actor who isn't exactly a household name would come into the show and deliver a brilliant performance.

D: As in the Season 2 classic, Lisa is embarrassed by her father and forever apologising for his behaviour, but by the end of the episode she learns that no man will ever love her more than he does. Homer's speech before the wedding about how proud he is of Lisa's accomplishments always reminds me of their conversation in her room after the 'baboon' incident, producing one of the sweetest moments of the season.

M: Another way that this season develops is the willingness to include greater influences from movies. I mean, there have always been great *moments* parodying famous films, but there are more and more entire slabs here that are direct tributes to film.

D: 'Itchy & Scratchy Land', for example?

M: Definitely, or the season opening 'Bart of Darkness' that is a fantastic parody of Hitchcock's *Rear Window*. 'Two Dozen and One Greyhounds' manages to play off both *101 Dalmations* AND *Beauty and the Beast* ... And then, of course, there is 'A Star is Burns' ...

D: 'A Star Is Burns' was apparently quite a controversial one for those who worked on the show. Groening reportedly saw it as being nothing more than an advertisement for *The Critic*, the show Jean and Reiss left *The Simpsons* to go make, and wanted so little to do with it that he actually had his name removed from the episode's credits.

M: While I could potentially see it being viewed that way, a little context goes a long way to explaining how this came about. The staff were still feeling the pinch of 25-episode seasons, to the point that Jean and Reiss brought their *Critic* staff over to help produce two episodes, namely this one and ''Round Springfield'.

D: Bringing them back in certainly gave us some classic moments. 'Man Getting Hit By Football' is without a doubt the greatest Hans Moleman moment of all time, made even funnier by Homer's reaction. Then we get Barney's 'Pukahontas', a cinematic masterpiece.

M: Let's not forget Steven Spielberg's Mexican counterpart: Señor Spielbergo. While 'A Star is Burns' is as packed with as many jokes as any episode in existence, took a heavier approach by killing off Bleeding Gums Murphy. Which, now that I think about the fact that they weren't working there any more, was a little presumptuous. But it did give us Lisa's rendition of 'Jazz Man', a song worth any price.

D: I like the different approach the writers took with Sideshow Bob in 'Sideshow Bob Roberts', switching up his role from bloodthirsty murderer to corrupt politician. He'd already failed twice at attempted murder, so it only made sense that a man of his intellect would have identified that he needed a new game plan. Writers Oakley and Weinstein based most of the episode on the Watergate scandal, with a number of other US political references also sprinkled throughout, not to mention movie parodies such as Bob's *A Few Good Men* speech in the courtroom.

M: It joins the great pieces of political satire in American entertainment. Watching the crowds lap up Bob's charisma despite not imparting any real message only feels more relevant today.

D: It's episodes like this that make me realise *The Simpsons* is responsible for me knowing more about American politics than I do about politics in my own country.

M: You do at least know that our Prime Minister isn't called Andy, right?

D: Yes. But I did once have a member of parliament named Gus.

M: We've barely scratched the surface of how many great episodes are on offer here, but I think we agree that this is the absolute peak of their run. Even if we both have personal favourites for different reasons, from a purely critical standpoint Season 6 is hard to go past.

D: While they were at the top of the moment, It was around this time that Groening was pitching for a live-action sitcom based on Krusty the Clown, in fact it even got to the stage where a pilot episode was written. I get how that might not have worked in 1994, but just imagine if Netflix suddenly decided to pick up *Krusty* starring Dan Castellaneta. It would send *Simpsons* fans into an absolute frenzy.

M: That may have been for the best, however. Not long after *Krusty* was shelved, Groening started development on *Futurama*.

'Bart vs. Australia'
(Season 6, Episode 16)
In Conversation

After placing a collect-call to Australia that costs $900 in order to disprove Lisa, Bart is indicted for fraud. Faced with a choice between a public apology or five years in prison, the Simpsons head to Australia to try and mend international relations.

MITCH: To properly explain 'Bart vs. Australia', we first need to look at Australia from the outside to give an idea of why this episode was so exciting to *Simpsons* fans on the inside. Australia has a paradoxical sense of itself. We are proudly defiant about our culture and how we are perceived. The 'true blue, dinky-die, howzit-goinmate?' identity that was pushed overseas is at once rejected as cliché, and yet accepted as our way of life.

DANDO: It *is* weird how we react to that. It's like we accept it as a generalisation until it gets applied to us individually.

M: That pretty much sums it up. We hate being thought of as somebody who wrestles crocodiles, but we love the idea that we are all strong enough to wrestle crocodiles.

D: What stands out in my memory is that the build-up to the episode was so massive in Australia that even news programmes were reporting on it. I can't imagine what my parents must have thought at the time hearing Peter Hitchener discussing a cartoon, but to my friends and me it was ground-breaking. Suddenly I was bonding with kids I'd

189

barely spoken a word to prior, purely because of our mutual excitement for the episode.

M: Totally. Aside from the build-up to 'Who Shot Mr. Burns? Part Two', and maybe the *Seinfeld* finale, I can't think of a TV moment that had more hype in my lifetime. The day following this episode at school, I remember that my usual group of friends sharing quotes had tripled in size.

D: I guess that comes down to the fact that *The Simpsons* visiting Australia was as monumental for us down under as it was for the family themselves, since it was the first time in the show's history that they'd ever left the United States.

M: See, that hadn't dawned on me until now.

D: I wasn't aware of that at the time either, but as an Australian fan that's something I'm now very proud of. Think about it: in 1995 the show was at the height of its fame and could have selected anywhere to take the Simpsons on their first international holiday, but they chose us because of our laid-back sense of humour.

M: Why do you think that was?

D: I've always thought it was because of our laid-back sense of humour.

M: And we're far enough away that it doesn't matter if we get offended?

D: Yeah, maybe that, too.

M: Back to how big an occasion it was, I've always thought our relationship with the USA is akin to a dog with an owner that is a little too busy. When it comes to film and TV, at the very least, we are a nation of sycophants desperately hoping for recognition and a pat on the head. In that sense, to Simpsons fans in the 90s, 'Bart vs. Australia' was like our owner coming home with a bag full of toys, taking us to the park, and scratching our bellies for eight consecutive hours. It's the same appeal as when a touring rock band yells out the name of your town.

D: *They know who we are!*

M: Exactly!

D: Not only did it create a buzz in Australia that can still be heard to this day, but it also spawned its own set of trading cards known as 'The Simpsons Down-Under' which currently take pride of place on my wall. There was also a ride based around the episode at the now defunct FOX Studios theme park in Sydney, which featured a re-edited and re-animated version of 'Bart vs. Australia'. Unfortunately I've never been able to find the footage. These days the episode lives on through things such as the bootleg 'Booting Flags' that have become an Australia Day tradition, 'Tobias memes' on social media . . .

M: It just had such a big impact. I still have a hard time ordering a drink in Australia without hearing 'Beer it is.'

D: We even signed a petition to have our national currency changed from 'dollars' to 'dollarydoos'. It's all a testament to the love and appreciation us Australian fans have for the episode.

M: I think I signed that under seven different names. When I watch the episode now, while it deals in well-trod stereotypes of Australia as a backwater country, it doesn't feel offensive, or like it's coming from a place of ignorance.

D: The writers did such a great job of exaggerating the outside perception of our way of life that in the process they delivered a perception that we'd prefer people to believe. As a result, so many gags from 'Bart vs. Australia' have become instilled in our day-to-day lives, from 'knifey-spoony' to 'dollarydoos', these terms have become a generational nod to an experience we all shared growing up. Our parents had the moon-landing we had the mooning of the Australian Prime Minister.

M: There were some people who got their nose out of joint on airing, but I find it hard to believe that anyone with that reaction was a regular *Simpsons* viewer. It's hard to call out a show for making fun of your country when it makes fun of its own at every turn. It's also impossible to ignore the element of truth to the satire. When Lisa mentions the Wolumbaloo Dirt Monument, I had to quickly check if that was indeed a real thing.

D: Obviously there were some 'professionally offended' critics who took the satirical look at 'Aussie culture' at face value, but you know where those reviewers are? All dead. How you doing down there, fellas? Huh? Huh?

M: Would now be a good time to point out that this is a book, and that without hearing that in Krusty's voice it *may* be misconstrued?

D: Noted.

M: As time has gone on, it has become one of the most loved episodes down under. I actually think that time has given it an extra layer to enjoy.

D: One example of that for me is the scene where Bart makes phone calls around the world. It has become such a lovely trip down memory lane for those who lived in the 90s. There's a shot showing Bart using a corded phone, dialling a number he found in a phone book to a country he found using a globe. It wasn't a deliberate attempt to set up nostalgia, but 20 years on it sure does highlight how far we've come on a communication scale.

M: For me, the only negative about 'Bart vs. Australia' is that it comes to an end. I would love to see a sequel where we find out what happens with the koala hitching a ride to America on the helicopter. Perhaps if *The Simpsons* ever comes to an end, they could revisit this with a *Planet of the Apes* style takeover of America for their final episode.

What did we learn?

Don't order a hamburger in Rand McNally.

Dando's Top 5

#5
'Homer the Vigilante'
(Season 5, Episode 11)

Homer forms his own vigilante group to try and catch a mystery cat burglar who has recently started stealing from Springfield residents.

Springfield is a city whose fragile self-belief leaves it forever teetering on the brink of impulsive, 'quick-fix' decision-making, often resulting in a situation more detrimental than beneficial to resolving the issue at hand. What happens when they receive three million dollars? They build a monorail. What happens when a 10-year-old boy steals the head of Jebediah's statue? They hunt him down with fire and pitchforks. What happens when a serial thief, known simply as 'The Cat Burglar', continues to steal their most prized possessions? Heavy sack beatings go up by a staggering 900%.

In 'Homer the Vigilante', many of Springfield's long-standing problems are hilariously exploited: police incompetence, sensationalised news reporting, reacting before thinking and, importantly, a reliance on mob/vigilante justice. You could argue it's the only form of action these poor saps know how to take when fighting against even the slightest of challenges.

Granted, having someone break into your home would frighten even the best of us. However, the idea that a vigilante group, fronted by Homer Simpson of all people, would help bring an end to the madness is the perfect example of their closed-minded way of thinking. The staggering incompetence on display is one of the many reasons why I absolutely love this episode.

It manages to poke fun at a society's obsession with firearms and taking matters into its own hands. Through the antics of doorknob-wielding middle-aged men in outrageous outfits (seriously, Moe as a Kaiser German gets me every time) it highlights the most obvious problems with vigilante justice. Then, at the climax, it seamlessly blends in one of my favourite film parodies in the series' history: the hunt for the 'Giant T', a take on the classic film *It's A Mad, Mad, Mad, Mad World*.

While it may not be a murder mystery, the overriding story that drives 'Homer the Vigilante' is one I've always considered a predecessor to the classic 'Who Shot Mr. Burns?' in that both are essentially whodunnit mysteries. The key difference being that, unlike the Season 6 cliffhanger, writer John Swartzwelder didn't try too hard to keep the big reveal here a secret. In fact, the blatant silhouette of Molloy and his trademark moustache in the opening sequence put the viewer in the driver's seat of the investigation. It adds a layer of dramatic irony to the equation, as the episode almost becomes a pantomime whenever Molloy is onscreen, encouraging the viewer to shout 'He's behind you!'

Molloy, played to perfection by Sam Neill, is a man

whose ambitions and end goals are never truly explored. Was he just your average kleptomaniac, or was there a hidden agenda behind his thievery? I mean, what was he ever going to do with a stamp collection?

For me, Molloy is the result of what would happen if someone from the real world entered the bubble in which Springfield exists finding amusement by taking advantage of the dimwits that surround him. The only problem is that it was so easy that it became boring, hence he allowed himself to be captured in order to create the task of making his great escape. It would explain why Molloy remained so calm and collected when the angry mob burst into his room at the retirement home after Grampa put the pieces of the puzzle together, as obvious as they were. Congratulating his foes on tracking him down, Molloy almost escapes with nothing more than a simple apology; however, thankfully Chief Wiggum (somewhat uncharacteristically) does his job and arrests the Cat Burglar for the crimes which he committed.

Finding himself behind bars, Molloy decides to test the intelligence levels of his fellow Springfieldians one last time by nonchalantly mentioning a hidden treasure that he's buried under a 'Giant T', immediately piquing their interest. This clue proves far too difficult for Homer & co. to work out, resulting in a disappointed Molloy simply giving them all the exact address where they can find the loot.

What follows is a sequence that's almost worthy of an episode in itself. Kicking off with one of my favourite Marge moments of all time as she slides down the police station stairs and onto a motorcycle with Homer in the sidecar, this two minutes of hilarity puts a final stamp on the episode's emphasis of just how dumb Springfield truly is. Upon discovering nothing more than a letter from Molloy himself detailing how he's used his time to escape from prison, the townspeople remain so swept up in the moment that they continue to dig anyway under the orders of their mayor, who assumes that by doing so they're 'bound to find something'.

In an era when the show was beginning to venture out into 'wacky' territory, 'Homer the Vigilante' manages to ride the fine line between absurdity and believability, resulting in one of Swartzwelder's finest contributions to the series.

What did we learn?

Don't panic if you ever fall into a hole – simply dig up.

#4
'Lemon of Troy'
(Season 6, Episode 24)

After a group of Shelbyville children steal Springfield's lemon tree, Bart leads a gang into rival territory to reclaim it. Worried about the boys, Homer leads a gang of his own to find them. When their paths meet, they join forces to bring the lemon tree back to Springfield.

I've always been a sucker for a well-orchestrated heist film. *Heat*, *Snatch*, *Ocean's Eleven*, I love them all. They're fun, they're exciting, they're suspenseful, they're great stories to tell when told right, and with a little help from some good ol' fashioned town pride and a fruit tree, 'Lemon of Troy' produces one of my all-time favourites.

For me, what's always made this episode stand out from the pack is the way it finally takes viewers on a journey through Shelbyville, a town we'd heard so much about but knew so little. To be honest, its inhabitants are rather pretentious for a community who pride themselves on marrying their own cousins. However, I guess what they lack in moral substance they make up for in football skills – after all, they beat Springfield nearly half the time.

While most heists tend to revolve around cash or at least something of value, the heart of *this* story is a lemon tree, the difference being that Springfield is technically only stealing back what rightfully belonged to it. The fact that they are so passionate about something I consider so meaningless is what I love the most. In saying that, writer Brent Forrester does such a great job at building up the tree's importance that by the time Homer & co. escape the Shelbyville impound lot, even I genuinely feel a sense of achievement for them, as if having this tree makes Springfield a better town. That's the charm of 'Lemon of Troy' in a nutshell.

At its core, this is an episode about town pride, a theme that truly struck a chord with me as a child, particularly during Marge's 'this town is a part of us all' speech. Even to this day, as a diehard Geelong Cats supporter it's hard not to get swept up when she points out the Springfield Isotopes cap, since I've never been able to fully grasp how anybody could support a team from an opposing town (I'm looking at you, Mitch!). Perhaps it's the music cue, or maybe it's Marge's repetitiveness;

either way, that moment manages to make me fall in love with our home town every single time I watch it.

Up until this point in the series, nobody seemed to 'want' to live in Springfield. It was almost like their own personal prison with everybody serving a life sentence, so it was important to establish a reason for Bart to want to defend it, and who better to defend it against than his Shelbyville clone, Shelby. The confrontation between the two groups of kids perfectly encapsulates the kind of harmless banter you'd hear in the school-yard. 'I know you are, but what am I?' 'Takes one to know one!' Seriously, perfect.

It wouldn't surprise me if Forrester actually sought input from kids while writing this script. He creates such a sense of fear and the unknown as Bart and his friends are raiding Shelbyville, when in actuality they were never in any *real* danger. However, coming from experience, this type of scenario would feel like 'life or death' for any group of 10-year-olds.

When Shelby and his gang steal the lemon tree, it reminds of the time my best mate's bike got stolen by kids from a nearby suburb. Rather than seek help from our parents, my group of friends decided to live vicariously through this episode and set ourselves the goal of entering the unknown to retrieve said bike. Looking back, I was most certainly the Milhouse of the operation, for not only did I provide the walkie-talkies, but I was also good at hiding in bushes while everyone else did the dirty work. We never did find the bike, I'm not sure we even looked in the right suburb, but much like this episode, it was fun while it lasted.

After being stolen, the lemon tree became more than a source of sour fruit: it was now a symbol of their manhood.

Once thriving for all to see, this symbol of their pride was now being held captive by their most hated rivals. The icing on this episode's cake is the way both the kids and the adults of Springfield eventually join forces to bring down their enemy and reclaim their position in this rivalry's food chain. It's not often we are treated to seeing two generations of Springfieldians working together, which is a shame as it works so well. Remember 'Bart the General'?

In the end, it's Bart's street-smarts that leads Team Springfield to victory, which makes sense with it being such a Bart-centric story. His idea of parking the van in front of the hospital in order to get impounded was pure genius, once again reaffirming that there's more than meets the eye with this under-achiever.

It'd be foolish of me not to mention that I found a new reason to love this episode in 2016, as it helped spawn possibly the most famous *Simpsons* meme in years – the 'lemon' meme. If only the animators knew at the time that their drawings would still be setting trends two decades on.

Through childish banter and challenging one's masculinity, 'Lemon of Troy' gives us a story that can be appreciated on many levels. Like many earlier episodes, it proves that at their peak, *The Simpsons* couldn't be matched for providing characters and stories we could all live vicariously through. Whether you're Bart, Homer or even Milhouse, this show is a part of us all, a part of us all, A PART OF US ALL!

What did we learn?

Rocky V + Rocky II = Rocky VII.

#3
'Who Shot Mr. Burns?'
Parts One and Two

When Mr. Burns learns that Springfield Elementary has struck oil, he devises a scheme to steal it, and the riches it promises. The drilling operation forces the closure of Moe's Tavern, and an oil burst destroys Bart's treehouse and wounds Santa's Little Helper. Not finished with his evil bidding, Burns reveals a plot to permanently block out the sun, forcing all residents to rely on electricity 24/7. Not long after activating the blocker, Burns is shot in a back alley, sparking the greatest whodunnit mystery this side of Agatha Christie.

The first and only two-part episode remains one of the more unusual in the show's history. This 46 minutes of television became the cornerstone for an event that defined the peak of *The Simpsons'* impact on the world of pop culture.

Designed to replicate the 'Who Shot J.R.?' concept from classic 80s soap opera *Dallas*, 'Who Shot Mr. Burns?' went one step further by allowing fans to truly immerse themselves in the show with the 'Simpsons Mystery Sweepstakes', a contest that offered a prize to whoever could solve the case. Although nobody was successful (besides an apparently anonymous fan on an online forum), the concept opened the door to new forms of interactivity between viewers and writers, becoming one of the first programmes to combine the internet with elements of a television show. It would have thrived in today's TV podcast generation, encouraging viewer participation and engagement in ways like never before.

The fact that the culprit remained a mystery right up to the ending of *Part Two* actually speaks volumes to the quality of the writing. Many clues that helped point the finger were cleverly sprinkled throughout, yet they were still vague enough to make us question our theory on who pulled the trigger.

Viewers managed to narrow it down to several key suspects, although Maggie never got a mention, despite the fact that she too vents her anger at the town meeting. It's a subtle hint that remains my favourite clue of the entire episode. Whilst at the time it may have seemed unreasonable to believe a baby did it, by Season 6, anything was possible in Springfield.

Sure, in hindsight these clues may make it quite easy to put the pieces together, yet this doesn't detract from the sheer joy and charm of reminiscing about the time you put on your Sherlock Holmes hat and attempted to figure it out for yourself.

The episode does an incredible job of positioning Mr. Burns as an evil villain, even more than usual, by using his greed to intertwine several unique events that help establish many Springfield residents as potential suspects.

Beginning with the unfortunate discovery of the lifeless body of class pet, Superdude, Groundskeeper Willie is issued the task of giving the beloved lizard a proper burial, a privilege not even his father had. Whilst digging, Willie discovers an untapped oil well, immediately making Springfield Elementary the richest school in the state.

Once Mr. Burns catches wind of the new-found fortune, he goes against Smithers' wishes and insists on taking it for himself by draining the oil from his own rig, creating turmoil throughout the town: the school is once again poor, Tito Puente loses his job as music teacher, Santa's Little Helper is temporarily paralysed, Moe is forced to close his bar, Smithers is fired, the Retirement Castle is damaged, everyone yells, oh – and most importantly – Burns can't remember Homer's name. Finally, in perhaps his most supervillain-esque act of all time, Burns decides to block out the sun so that the town will be forever run on electricity sourced from the nuclear power plant. This is where the 'fun' begins.

Everything leading up to the inevitable shooting forms a well-placed seed plant that makes this episode so much more enjoyable on repeat viewing. As this aired before the internet was in every home, we were required to freeze-frame and actually find the clues ourselves, rather than learning them all with a quick Google search. By ending 'Part One' with Dr. Hibbert seemingly breaking the fourth wall and asking us if we can solve the mystery, it created the perfect set-up for one of television's greatest cliffhangers.

Season 7 kicked off with Burns' long-time assistant Smithers waking from a drunken binge, believing himself to be guilty and turning himself in. Looking back, Smithers was always a 'too obvious to be guilty' suspect, but that didn't stop eight-year-old Dando from thinking he'd solved the case, spending six months obnoxiously telling his sister Stacey that 'it's obviously Smithers'.

Soon enough we learn of Smithers' innocence, with the majority of the episode then spent crossing off the potential suspects one by one as their often laughable alibis are all checked out, including my personal favourite, the iconic lie detector test of Moe Szyslak.

It's no secret that for many the final reveal of Maggie as the infamous shooter left a bad taste in the mouth, including my own at the time. After all, how could a baby have the strength to aim a gun, let alone pull the trigger? These were just some of the questions I threw out in a fit of anger once the credits started rolling, partially because I was too young to appreciate the hilarity behind the absurdness of it all, but mostly because it meant that I was wrong.

These days it'd be near-impossible to find anyone under the age of 40 who hasn't watched this episode, or who is at least unaware of who in fact shot Mr. Burns. It was such a historic moment in television history that it was THE topic of water-cooler discussions for the week following. However, if by a miraculous chance you do find somebody who, still oblivious to the hysteria, don't pass on the chance to sit them down and watch along as they too try and crack the case, living vicariously through them as you once again enjoy one of *The Simpsons'* crowning achievements.

What did we learn?

Babies in Texas better not shoot anybody.

#2
'The Springfield Files'
(Season 8, Episode 10)

After getting lost on his way home from Moe's after a heavy drinking session, Homer has an encounter with an extraterrestrial. Only Bart believes his story, with even Agents Mulder and Scully unable to find any evidence to support Homer's claim. After Bart manages to capture another encounter on tape, the whole town becomes convinced and sets up camp the following Friday. Only Lisa remains a sceptic, and is ultimately proven correct when the 'alien' turns out to be Mr. Burns.

From a young age, I've always loved science fiction. Many hours of my youth were spent sitting in front of the television watching films such as *E.T.*, *The Empire Strikes Back*; hell, even *Mac and Me* was on regular rotation. The only issue was that none of my friends shared the same love for aliens and lightsabres. They all looked at the genre the same way people look at me when I tell them I'm still a wrestling fan at the age of 29. I remember questioning why I seemed to be the only person I knew who was interested in seeing Yoda lift an X-Wing out of the water with nothing but his mind, then 'The Springfield Files' came along and I realised that I was not alone.

This was the first time *The Simpsons* had dedicated an entire episode to parodying another one of FOX's hit programmes, providing us with an abundance of sci-fi references in the form of an episode of *The X-Files*. From Chewbacca singing 'Good Morning Starshine' while wearing a 'Homer Is A Dope' shirt, to a police line-up featuring the likes of Alf and Marvin the Martian, 'The Springfield Files' was a 22-minute showcase for the writers to overindulge in their inner geek. In the process, they reaffirmed to 9-year-old Dando that he wasn't out of touch for enjoying science fiction, it was the children who were wrong.

What's always made me laugh is that showrunner Al Jean actually thought of the idea for this episode while sitting on the toilet. He saw *The X-Files* on the cover of *TV Guide* and knew it would make for a fun parody. It was a bold concept that many of the writers initially rejected, but that didn't stop Jean and Mike Reiss from delivering a brilliant mash-up. What stands out is that the script celebrates *The X-Files* just as much as it pokes fun at it. This wasn't like the dismissive parody of *Married with Children* in 'Deep Space Homer', this was a crossover that fans of both shows could appreciate. Even Agent Mulder's photo of himself in a Speedo, which may seem like nothing more than a funny visual to non-*X-Files* viewers, is actually a direct reference to the episode 'Duane Barry', in which David Duchovny wore only a Speedo. These subtle in-jokes for *X-Files* fans were crucial to the episode's success since at the time of airing, *The X-Files* was one of television's most popular programmes. In fact just two weeks later, *The X-Files* episode 'Leonard Betts' became the highest-rated in the show's history. Some say that was because it followed Super Bowl XXXI, but I like to believe it was due to the buzz generated by 'The Springfield Files'.

Kicking off with Leonard Nimoy introducing us to the story (in a parody of his programme *In Search Of . . .*) immediately sets the tone that this won't be your average episode. Much like the 'Treehouse of Horror' series, extraordinary events will occur that should be treated as non-canon. It fitted the vibe of the *X-Files* motif and allowed viewers to suspend their disbelief when the alien revealed to be Mr. Burns all along. Credit must also be given to Nimoy, who delivered an even more memorable performance here than he did in 'Marge vs. the Monorail'. The best guest stars are always the ones who are willing to embrace the absurdity that comes with visiting Springfield.

Given the amount of sci-fi references and parodies throughout, I've always looked at this episode as the closest thing we got to *Futurama* before the show actually launched in 1999. With *Futurama* being set in the future, the writers had more freedom to push the boundaries a little more than they could on *The Simpsons*, resulting in the type of story we get in 'The Springfield Files'. Although I must admit that some of my favourite references in the episode aren't even sci-fi related. Homer's retelling of *Speed* as 'The Bus That Couldn't Slow Down' is a perfect example of the *Simpsons* writing staff in their prime.

Aside from the guest appearances and sci-fi spoofs, the driving force of the episode is Homer's determination to prove he's not insane. Nobody believes his story, not even Marge, the one person who has always supported him whether she agrees or not. Granted, if someone with Homer's track record turned up half-sober claiming to have seen an alien, I'd find it hard to swallow his story myself. Still, as a viewer you *want* Homer to succeed because you know he's telling the truth. When Bart reveals that he believes his father, it's a nice moment of support that we rarely get to see from him without any ulterior motive. Just like me when I first watched this episode, he's a young boy who wants to believe in the existence of life in outer space. After all, what kid would pass up the opportunity to see a real-life alien?

'The Springfield Files' may not appear in the Top 5 for most fans. While I'm sure it can be enjoyed purely for Homer's crazy shenanigans, having knowledge of *The X-Files*, as well as the movies and characters which it satirises, adds an extra layer of hilarity that raises its glass to the geek community. This was written for those of us willing to line up for hours to secure a good seat at a *Star Wars* midnight screening, for those of us who never really grew up, for those of us who choose to believe.

What did we learn?

The truth is out there.

#1
'22 Short Films About Springfield' (Season 7, Episode 21)

In a series of short scenes, we get a glimpse of the many stories of the many lives being lived out in Springfield.

Without question, '22 Short Films About Springfield' is my all-time favourite episode. Based loosely on Quentin Tarantino's 1994 hit film *Pulp Fiction*, it incorporates one of the more unusual structures in the series' history by intertwining a number of different stories starring some of the show's favourite secondary characters. By its seventh season *The Simpsons* had developed the largest cast on television, but more impressively almost all of these characters were capable of carrying a story on their own. Whether it's Dr. Nick saving Grampa from a dangerous case of *bonus eruptus*, or Comic Book Guy wheeling and dealing for the sake of 75 cents, no episode does a better job of showcasing the extensive universe of Springfield.

'22 Short Films' certainly isn't for everybody. If you prefer stories with structure that lead to an emotional payoff then you're certainly not going to find that here.

What you do get though is 23 minutes of short, sharp hilarity that emphasise just how far the show had come by 1996. It may have still been called *The Simpsons* but the Simpsons were no longer the only stars of the show; everyone was important in their own right from Bumblebee Man all the way to the Very Tall Man. The Simpson family still play a role in this episode but they certainly weren't relied upon like usual. In fact Homer only appears for a little over a minute, which, as funny as that segment is (I've always loved the fact that he somehow had his quarters run over by a train, yet decided to keep them anyway), has got to be some kind of record.

Besides *The Simpsons Movie*, this episode had more credited writers than any other *Simpsons* project in history, which is understandable considering just how much is going on. There truly is never a dull moment as Jim Reardon's directing ensures each story ends with a direct transition into the next. In fact, the way it flows from one story to the next, it almost feels like you're watching a living comic strip. Nothing outstays its welcome, with some segments getting more airtime than others where required. A classic example of this is the 'steamed hams' segment starring Principal Skinner and Superintendent Chalmers, which was written by then-showrunner Bill Oakley.

This scene is unique in the way it was scripted, coming across more like a conversation between Jerry and George at Monks in *Seinfeld* than a conversation we'd expect to hear on *The Simpsons*. This was a show that never wasted a single line of dialogue; everything had to be either a punchline, setting up a punchline or furthering the story, but what we get here is Skinner and Chalmers discussing nothing of any real substance since it's all a lie anyway. It wouldn't surprise me if a lot of this was improvised by Castellaneta and Shearer, it's just the little things like Chalmers saying 'of course' as Skinner goes to check on his kitchen. I think that's what makes this such a memorable moment because it feels like *real* people having a *real* conversation. Even visually there's not a lot going on until the aurora borealis breaks out in Skinner's kitchen, it's just one man trying to convince the other that he is telling the truth, by covering up one outlandish lie with another. Shearer's acting is amazing as he lies with enough conviction to fool a man who would normally be able to see right through Skinner's shenanigans.

It's a similar situation with Chief Wiggum's conversation about McDonald's with Eddie and Lou at Krusty Burger, a reference to Vincent and Jules' 'royal with cheese' discussion in *Pulp Fiction*. No other episode would allow for three characters to waste so much time comparing 'Krusty partially-gelatinated non-dairy-gum-based beverages' to 'shakes', but it just fits so well here. What's so great about it is that it holds up even if you haven't seen *Pulp Fiction*, as most of my generation wouldn't have when this went to air, but for those who have it's a fitting tribute that makes all Tarantino fans smile with glee.

My favourite segment in the entire episode is actually a direct parody of one of *Pulp Fiction's* most iconic scenes involving gimps and torture. Herman was the perfect replacement for Maynard, ensuring we could never look at him the same way again. The shot of Chief Wiggum and Snake tied to chairs and beaten is a visual that I think is quite possibly one of the darkest moments in *The Simpsons*, especially when you know what evil intentions Herman had planned for them next. Thankfully

Milhouse saves the day in the most ironic reference of them all, accidentally 'going medieval' on Herman.

The original idea for '22 Short Films' was actually spawned by the 'Adventures of Ned Flanders' clip at the end of Season 4's 'The Front'. It was a standalone clip that existed within its own bubble and had no bearing on the episode it was attached to. This is a format I'm surprised the show hasn't used more often, since I've always believed it could have evolved into an annual tradition much like the 'Treehouse of Horror' series. At the time there were even talks of creating a separate spin-off series titled Springfield Stories, which would focus on the town as a whole as opposed to just the Simpson family. We may be in Season 29 but it's certainly not too late to try something fresh, especially since some of the best episodes from later seasons have been those that break the usual format, like 'Trilogy of Error', 'The Seemingly Never-Ending Story' and '24 Minutes'.

'22 Short Films About Springfield' may lack the standard formula that made *The Simpsons* a television icon, but there's still a freshness to it that makes it stand out from the pack even to this day. It's almost got a season's worth of classic moments within one episode, many of which I didn't have room for in this review, although that's a testament to just how fantastically produced it really is. It gives Springfield an identity by offering us a fly-on-the-wall guided tour in real time. We as fans will never get the opportunity to visit this crazy town, but watching '22 Short Films' is absolutely the next best thing.

What did we learn?

Everyone needs to drive a vehicle, even the very tall.

An Interview with Bill Oakley

After starting on the show as a writer in Season 4, Bill Oakley quickly found himself thrust into a position of seniority due to a mass change of staff. Quickly proving himself capable of both paying tribute to the style of episodes that had come before him, as well as showing an ability to experiment with new formats, Bill found himself running the show with Josh Weinstein by the time Season 7 rolled around. We spoke with Bill about coming into the show in a time of change, and what makes certain characters tick.

You and Josh Weinstein were the first 'fans' to be hired on the writing team. Do you think that helped you both to think like a fan and produce the type of stories that we all wanted?

I think it's a slight exaggeration to say that we were the first 'fans' to be hired, since I'm sure Conan would have been a fan, but perhaps not the kind of fan that *we* were in terms of what you'd call a '*Simpsons* nerd'. I mean we collected *Simpsons* merchandise and even wrote for *The Simpsons Comics* before we got on the staff, so if anything, I'd say we were bigger nerds than anybody else in terms of Simpsonology.

To answer your question though, I don't think we were really thinking about it in terms of doing shows that appeal to the fans. We were trying to do shows that *we* liked. Everybody says this about TV, but the kiss of death is trying do stuff that will appeal to the audience as opposed to doing what you think is great and hoping the audience will like it. For the most part during our time there, including when we were working under Mike and Al and then David Mirkin, we were all just trying to do shows that *we* thought were really amusing and everybody else was collateral.

When first starting out as writers, what unique elements do you think yourself and Josh were able to bring to the table?

I don't believe that we brought a unique spin to the show as much as a desire to be faithful to what we thought its tenets were. We didn't come into the show saying 'We're gonna do it our way!' we were more like 'We're gonna do it just like they did before.' When we did Season 7, we literally sat down and copied Season 3, which I still say is the best season of television ever made, and we weren't even there for it. We worked out that they did six Homer episodes; one Sideshow Bob, one Itchy & Scratchy, two Lisa episodes, etc., and we patterned our work on Season 3. The stories were different but our idea was to reproduce what we considered to be the gold. The only thing that we changed was that we allowed two episodes per season that were incredibly self-indulgent format-bending stuff like '22 Short Films About Springfield' and 'The Simpsons Spin-Off Showcase'. We thought the show was going to be over by Season 9, or 10 at the latest, so we figured why not have some fun with this thing? You know, 'Nobody's paying attention, nobody tells us what to do so let's just do what we want to.' That was how '22 Short Films' came about.

Well, '22 Short Films' is Dando's personal favourite, along with some other format-bending episodes. Did you ever think of any other concepts that didn't fit the show at the time but might have in later seasons?
I feel like Josh and I, along with our staff, were almost running out of ideas by the end of Season 8, so I don't believe there were many things we didn't do that we had wanted to. As I said, back then it was a rare, practically unique situation in the history of television where we were able to broadcast the show and nobody was paying any attention. Due to the nature of the deal with FOX, they weren't allowed to give us any notes or do anything other than broadcast the show. Jim Brooks, who was the *real* boss of the show, was off directing his movies for several years during that time, so we didn't see him very much either. Josh and I were able to be as self-indulgent as we wanted. It's interesting because at the time I don't think people liked '22 Short Films' all that much. I don't think they liked Frank Grimes much at the time either. However, what happened was it became a self-fulfilling prophecy where the kids who were watching it at the time grew into the kind of fans who *would* appreciate those episodes.

Frank Grimes is the most real character we've ever seen on the show, like somebody from the real world being thrown into the insanity of Springfield. Besides giving Homer an enemy, what were your main intentions with the Grimes character and what did he represent?
To take a step back for a minute, another idea that we were surprised we came up with was when Homer became Mr. Burns' assistant in 'Homer the Smithers' – we couldn't believe it hadn't already been done. With

213

Frank Grimes we were just trying to come up with various things on TV shows and one of those things was that a character usually has an enemy. Characters had wanted to kill Homer in the past but he's never had someone who was morally opposed to him. So we wondered, 'What would that person be like?' Well, he'd be a real rule-following guy who had the opposite personality to Homer. The other thing that we added was that he would seem like he'd come from the real world, commenting on things that everyone had taken for granted for so long, like Homer being the chief safety inspector at the power plant. Obviously it was made up as a joke in Season 1, but after eight years somebody could easily point out how horrifying it is that he's responsible for our safety. So we just decided to have Frank come in and question all the assumptions that everyone had had about Homer for all this time.

You guys joined the show during a transitional period where many of the original writers were leaving for other projects. Were you disappointed knowing you wouldn't be working with this legendary group for much longer, or was it seen as more of an opportunity for you both?
It was disappointing initially but then David Mirkin came in and built a new staff. The collateral benefit of that was that we became the most senior guys on the show after having been there for only nine months. So it was an opportunity for us since I think we got bumped up around four levels almost immediately to supervising producer. Also because of our *Simpsons* 'nerdery', we

were also, well, I wouldn't say we were directing for those two years because David was, but he did let us write five episodes each season and they went on the air without too much adjustment.

Can you remember the first idea either of you pitched?
It was the gambling episode '$pringfield'. We pitched it during the weird twilight-zone era where some of the original guys were still there at the retreat, including Sam Simon. That was actually the last time we saw Sam working on the show, it was he, Mike, Al and a number of the original writers right before they all left. After that we had a weird period on the show where nobody was running it for like two months; the only writing employees were myself, Josh, Conan and Dan McGrath. We were just writing all these episodes on our own until Mirkin got hired.

On the topic of '$pringfield', growing up in Australia Howard Hughes wasn't really on our radar until The Aviator came out. So Burns suddenly going crazy and bottling his own urine came from left field for us. Was that in the original pitch, or was that just bouncing things around in a room and that's where it got to?
That was part of the original pitch because it fit so perfectly. Howard Hughes was this casino magnet who lived on the top floor of his casino in Las Vegas as he gradually went crazy, and it just seemed natural for Burns to start his own casino and slowly turn into Hughes. It was honestly one of the first ideas we had for that episode.

You mentioned '22 Short Films' earlier, and you've gone on record saying that Chalmers is one of your favourite characters. We were wondering how long the 'Steamed Hams' segment took to write because every line in that is so refined and there's not a wasted syllable.

It took an afternoon for me to write. I'm sure you've heard the story of how it originated from the 'Adventures of Ned Flanders' clip at the end of 'The Front'. We always just thought that was so funny and the reason they did that was because the episode came in short. We never had that problem; in fact our episodes always came in too long. So finally someone just came up with the bright idea of let's just do a whole episode with those shorts and tie them all together. It was around the time *Pulp Fiction* came out and we realised we could have a story that wove them. I remember we got to choose our three favourite characters and then drew one out of a hat. I really wanted to write for Chalmers because I loved all those moments that came before where Skinner would lie and Chalmers would reject briefly and then believe it. I wanted to do a whole sequence of those things, it took a while to come up with the idea but then it all unfolded quite quickly.

The thing about that sequence is that there aren't any traditional 'jokes' in there, like Homer getting hit on the head and yelling 'Doh!' or Bart prank-calling Moe. I was actually afraid when I did it that people would say there's nothing funny about it, because it's just 13 inter-connected lies that become more and more preposterous as opposed to traditional jokes.

It's very straight-faced, like the line 'it's an Albany expression', for example.

Yeah, that's why I'm surprised it's taken off like it has and become so popular over the years. Again this is the perfect example of the show having a second life due to the internet, since I don't remember anybody talking about 'steamed hams' for at least the first ten years after it aired. I don't recall anybody even noticing it at all and it's only with the Internet and the way it's taken on a meme life of its own that it's finally taken off.

Do you think it might be that people have become more accustomed to watching TV comedy without laugh tracks? That's a scene where a traditional sitcom audience might need to be told where to laugh, whereas shows like Arrested Development *and* Community *have helped people learn to find the jokes themselves?*
I think that's definitely possible, that nowadays a large proportion of people are willing to appreciate comedy that doesn't have traditional set-up/punchline rhythms.

Jumping to another one of your more famous episodes, 'Who Shot Mr. Burns?' *As someone who wrote the script, what was it like watching the hysteria you caused over that summer?*
There really wasn't any hysteria; it's another classic example of the pre- and post-internet world. The internet wasn't predominant back then so we didn't hear anything. We knew that FOX was spending a lot of money to promote it and putting things up in 7/11, which was rare for them to do at the time, but there was really no way for us to know if people were interested. All we knew was that FOX was interested enough to make it a whole night of programming; even then I'm

not sure it was in the Top 20 rated shows for that week. Again though, it's now taken on a life of its own. My guess is that these days nobody knows what other shows were airing that week, but they still remember when they watched 'Who Shot Mr. Burns?'

It's funny that you say there was no hysteria because as a kid, we were roughly eight years old at the time, it was all we were talking about in the schoolyard. It really was a big deal to us.
That's really cool, but we had no idea. The only way we knew what people were thinking was if they wrote us a letter. We'd occasionally look at *Simpsons* forums, but that was a rarefied group of people who usually hated everything that we loved, so we couldn't take it too seriously.

The fact that you had the dial-up modem installed in your office just so you could read the forums like alt. simpsons clearly shows that you cared what the fans were thinking. Did you ever read anything in those forums that inspired an idea for an episode?
No, not really, we had to be very careful about that. I don't remember ever reading many ideas for episodes being pitched in the forums, and if I did I'd immediately ignore it because I didn't want to be accused of stealing someone's notion for an episode. I've said before that my interest in it declined as time went by because it just became more aggravating than amusing. It was enjoyable to read when I was just a *Simpsons* fan who was a low-level guy on the show, I actually felt a sense of camaraderie as we were all posting about the episodes. Then

the more I became involved with the episodes and started producing them, seeing people's blisteringly negative reactions to them online became upsetting and I had the modem removed from my office.

You've said that 'the new guy always gets the Marge episodes', which is why Jean and Reiss assigned you and Josh to 'Marge Gets a Job'. When did you first feel like you were no longer 'the new guy' and felt like you 'belonged' at The Simpsons?
It happened really quickly because not long after we started, eleven people left the show. So we went from being literally the newest guys in June of '92, then in November of '92 we were the second-newest guys, and then six months later Conan left and we were the most senior guys on the show.

It's amazing that so much change didn't bring about an entire season of Marge episodes . . .
Well, the result of having so many new people was that we suddenly got to write the Homer episodes. Back then the Homer episodes were the gold that you only gave to George Meyer, Jon Vitti or Swartzwelder, then all of a sudden, the very first one we wrote for Season 5 was '$pringfield', which was Mr. Burns and Homer primarily.

In regard to Homer, from a writer's perspective, it feels like with that character you can draw parallels to Bugs Bunny in that depending on who's writing and directing him, Homer can go many different ways. He can be overly aggressive towards Bart, sometimes he's beyond

219

dim-witted, yet other times he's quite clever with his schemes. What is your quintessential version of Homer?
I think Homer is essentially a well-meaning boob. I never liked it when Homer became mean or vindictive because ultimately he has a good soul and a good heart. Swartzwelder once said that the best way to write Homer was as a big, enthusiastic dog. He couldn't really control his desire to eat or know when to rest when he was tired, but still he was so lovable. That was the way we always loved to write him, then when we were head writers we forced others to write him that way also.

We always thought that on the rare occasion when Homer was shown to be genuinely good at something, that it was super-enjoyable. In 'Lisa the Iconoclast' when Homer becomes the town crier, he's really good at it and we really loved that. Having Homer have a couple of wins now and then was always really satisfying and showed that he was in fact good for something once in a while.

We couldn't agree more – with 'Dancing Homer' in particular, which is the first time we see him genuinely successful and have a lot of people behind what he does. It was uplifting to go back and watch that from a more critical point of view and actually take note of what was happening onscreen.
Yeah that episode is really great. It's also quite realistic in a way with the way it all unfolds, when you think about it.

Growing up, we struggled to relate to the character of Lisa, however the older we got the more we realised that we both are Lisa. When you were writing the show, which character do you think you related to the most?

220

If we're talking about the family, I'd have to say Lisa with a little bit of Bart and Homer mixed in. However, if we're talking about the universe of Springfield it's definitely Chalmers, that's why I love him so much. I remember we took a poll in the writers' room back in the day and ten of the twelve writers, including Matt Groening, said that *Green Acres* was their favourite show, growing up. I tend to think Eddie Albert in *Green Acres* and Chalmers are similar in the sense that they were unlike anybody else on the show. They'd be putting up with a lot of crazy people who didn't really know what they were doing but they just had to muddle their way through. That's what Chalmers is all about. He and Hibbert are the only sane guys in this whole town, but in order to function they have to simply write it off. Chalmers knows everyone's lying, he knows everyone's bad at their job, but he only cares enough just to ask one question and then he moves along because otherwise he'd lose his mind. I guess that's me in a way.

Were there any characters that you had a hard time writing for?
There are various things that are hard to write, like when Groundskeeper Willie calls people names such as 'croquet playing mint-munchers', those kinds of things take time. Sideshow Bob was difficult for the same reason – just characters that have a really complicated way of speaking. I'd also have to say Bart because he's hard to make funny in a non-corny way. Writing Homer and Lisa is pretty easy. Actually, Marge is quite easy too, even though it's not much fun because she doesn't have a lot of crazy personality flaws. Bart is difficult

since you're expecting him to be original and witty, as well as a prankster while also having some relatable emotions. I certainly wouldn't want to be assigned a Bart episode if it was my first day on the job there because it's so hard to do it right.

One of the keys to Bart is that when it's done really well, he might have the wit of an older kid but the emotions or logic of a 10-year-old. For example, when Lisa's trying to figure out if he's smarter than a hamster, the lines he says are funny and beyond his years, yet he's still going to keep touching an electrified cupcake.

Yep for sure, that type of stuff was always hard to do. Jon Vitti was really good at treading that line, but also managed to keep it from being corny.

Speaking of Bart, your episode 'Bart vs. Australia' is something we all hold very dear to our hearts. It was a phenomenon when it aired and to this day it's incredibly popular.

Cool! I just watched that last night, actually and I've always been curious about what people in Australia thought about that episode. I remember we got hundreds of letters from angry schoolchildren from Australia asking us why we treated their country so poorly. Obviously, it'd been some sort of school assignment. So really the only response we ever got from Australia was a bunch of angry letters from kids.

It's weird that so many kids would say they didn't like it. When it aired, every kid at our schools absolutely loved it.

I'm so glad to hear that. You know, it was all just cobbled together from the corniest stereotypes from Australia, and we always knew the show was big down there so we thought Australians would get a kick out of it. Also, part of the joke is that Australia is treated as such an assemblage of stereotypes and we just kept heaping them on, we literally took every opportunity. Even the guys in parliament who are all such hillbillies, it's so funny. It's the stereotypes that Australia has exported to the world being reflected back in our vision of the country.

Anyway, as I said, I'm so happy to hear that it was appreciated in the spirit in which we wrote it.

Forgive me for putting you on the spot, but what was your favourite episode prior to working on the show?
Before I got on the show my favourite was always 'Radio Bart' and I know that nobody ever picks that one . . .

That's actually in Mitch's Top 5 in this book . . .
Wow! Fantastic. Well, you and I are clearly simpatico. It's not one of those ones that stands out as super-memorable like 'Lisa's Substitute' or 'Homer the Heretic', mainly because Season 3 was so perfect that an episode like 'Radio Bart' can easily fly under the radar. That's really a testament to how amazing the rest of the episodes were, like 'Homer at the Bat'. The thing is, people always remember the ones with all the gimmicks, but 'Radio Bart' is honestly the perfect *Simpsons* episode from A to Z. It had a ton of hilarious, well-observed gags about society, going to Chuck E. Cheese or even the social phenomenon when a kid's fallen down the

well. Then there's the song 'Sendin' Our Love Down the Well' with a celebrity appearance from Sting – it had everything that you would want from a classic *Simpsons* episode. If you explain the top 10 things that made *The Simpsons* so great, this episode had all of them. It doesn't stick in people's minds because it's not gimmicky like the baseball one, yet it's the apex of the show's creative abilities.

Which writer from the original team did you most admire?
Of the people I worked with, George Meyer is the best TV comedy writer of all time. To vastly oversimplify it, he's incredibly perceptive and has the most jaundiced take on modern American society. He observes things about society that most of us take for granted. Similar to how Frank Grimes reacts when he first arrives at the power plant, that's the way George reacts to modern American society. George was the backbone of the show for all the years he was there.

Which episode would you say best describes working on the show?
At the risk of sounding obvious I'd have to say 'The Itchy & Scratchy & Poochie Show'. I think we made it very clear to the viewer exactly what it was like and the frustrations one would experience. Fortunately, we never actually got forced to add the character of Roy or someone similar to the show, but that episode combined with 'The Front' is pretty illustrative of what it was like to work on *The Simpsons*.

Season 7 (1995-96)
In Conversation

DANDO: Without question, this is my favourite season of the series. Everybody I knew was watching the show by this point, whether it be religiously or casually. We were all coming down from the high of the 'Who Shot Mr. Burns?' hysteria, but by no means were the season's remaining episodes riding on its coat-tails. From my personal favourite '22 Short Films About Springfield' to the muumuu-induced 'King-Size Homer', this season truly has it all.

MITCH: I don't remember ever anticipating a season as much as I did in the lead-up to 'Who Shot Mr. Burns? (Part 2)'. I remember the lead-in was a special episode of *America's Most Wanted*, dubbed 'Springfield's Most Wanted'. The idea that a true crime show would dedicate half an hour to my favourite cartoon was mind-blowing, and one of the few times I remember everybody in my family huddled around the TV with bated breath. Fortunately, the season lived up to the hype.

D: This was the first season under Executive Producers Bill Oakley and Josh Weinstein, who had both actually been working on the show since Season 3. I love the dynamic they brought, particularly with the way they wanted to break the format with episodes such as '22 Short Films', 'The Simpsons 138th Episode Spectacular' and 'Who Shot Mr. Burns?' (Parts One and Two).

225

M: With a lot of shows, particularly sitcoms, the writing staff tends to change every few years. So you get this evolution where if the show is successful enough, people start working on it who were fans of it before they came on. With a show like *The Simpsons* it means that later seasons turn into an interpretation of sorts of what the current staff liked about the episodes that came before. Luckily for us, Oakley and Weinstein were able to naturally blend their own style and voice with what came before. They clearly loved where the show came from, and managed to keep in step with the past while finding ways to push into the future.

D: Another moment that received huge hype this year came with the annual instalment of 'Treehouse of Horror'.

M: Well, talk about ways of pushing into the future. The 3D animation in 'Hom3r' was ground-breaking for its time. I mean, this aired before *Toy Story* was released, so 3D animation was new ground.

D: I remember being disappointed that the whole episode wasn't in 3D because of how heavily it was promoted in the lead-up.

M: I was also a little bit thrown off, thinking that they'd played the wrong episode for a while by mistake.

D: You mentioned Oakley and Weinstein's ability to blend the old with the new. I think the best example of that is in 'Mother Simpson'. Homer gazing up at the stars during the closing credits is one of the most iconic visuals in the history of the series. No matter how many times you watch it there's just no cure for the impact of that moment's raw emotion.

M: In such a rapid-fire show that never feels like it's sitting still, it's rare for such a quiet moment of beauty to be allowed to stand for so long. It has shades of the

Futurama episode 'Jurassic Bark'. It's moments like these that continued to elevate the show above all competitors.

D: It's even now taken on a new life of its own, quite often used as a meme when a much-loved celebrity passes away. Interestingly, I'd never really given much thought to the fact that Homer's mother hadn't been addressed by this point, besides a couple of brief appearances in flashback sequences.

M: You're right. You would have thought it would be a question posed much earlier in the show's run . . . maybe they had never figured out the way to tell the story until now. Or, maybe given the age and relative irrelevance of Grampa, it was just easier to ignore for a while. Either way, given that we've known Homer for such a long time, it helps sell Homer's confusion and despair at never having known his mother. If this story was told in Season 2, for example, it wouldn't have had the extra weight of our shared history to fall back on.

D: I love watching Homer practically become a boy again, making up for the childhood he never had by trying to impress Mona with handstands.

M: Mona's arrival was also quite a breakthrough for Lisa. It provided an explanation for the source of Lisa's intelligence, finally giving her a relative of equal intellect to engage with.

D: As a child, I always loved the concept of 'Bart on the Road', envisioning myself in Bart's shoes as I decided where I'd go and who I'd take along for the ride. I never had the courage to attempt such a thing, the one time I threatened to run away from home only resulted in me hiding up a tree in the front yard for two hours, wondering why nobody had come looking for me.

M: For me, it was 'Radioactive Man' that I desperately wanted to be my own life. The concept of open

227

auditions felt like it would be my ticket to stardom. I remember buying a local paper when I was about eight to see if any were being held nearby, which was admittedly an ambitious wish, living on the opposite side of the planet to Hollywood. I must have read . . . maybe half of a classified section before getting distracted by a video game, and the dream was over.

D: This season gave us our first and only real insight into the personal life of the unforgettable (and irreplaceable) Troy McClure with 'A Fish Called Selma'. While McClure felt like a regular member of the cast, up until now we'd only ever experienced him in small doses, which is a shame because this episode is proof that the character was more than capable of holding a story on his own. Hartman's incredible performance in *Stop the Planet of the Apes! I Want to Get Off!* is without question my favourite musical moment in the series; Dr. Zaius, lasers, breakdancing apes and a piano solo, that play had everything.

M: I shudder to think of the sum of money I'd be willing to part with to buy a ticket to see this in real life. Given that Troy had never had any personal interaction with the main characters before, he really does feel like a celebrity here. *The Simpsons* so often puts its characters in fish-out-of-water scenarios, but here, the audience are the fish, lapping up the life of celebrity . . . and if Fat Tony is to be believed, sleeping with Troy himself.

D: Homer takes up two of my favourite sports in this season, the first being golf in 'Scenes from the Class Struggle in Springfield' and ten pin bowling in 'Team Homer'. Strangely enough Mr. Burns plays the antagonist in both stories; however rather than being his usual evil self, it's more a case of Smithers hiding him from the reality of his poor athletic ability.

M: Smithers is the ultimate yes-man. I love that Burns genuinely has no idea that he isn't a golfing prodigy.

D: I think every *Simpsons* fan has referred to golf balls as reptile eggs at least once in their life, while personally I've never gone a whole round without referring to my 'open-faced club sandwich', which probably says more about my golfing skills than anything else.

M: This was also the season where the show finally got its ultimate revenge on George Bush for his 'More like the Waltons, less like the Simpsons' line. 'Two Bad Neighbors' was another example of the show's confidence that virtually any scenario would be bought into by its fans.

D: That was also the first episode to feature Disco Stu. Bill Oakley considers 'Two Bad Neighbors' a companion piece to 'Homer's Enemy', where they've essentially dropped a real person into the crazy world of Springfield.

M: Not making the episode political and essentially turning Bush into a stand-in for Mr. Wilson helps keep the episode a timeless classic. Oddly, though, despite all the back and forth between the Simpsons and Bushes, Skinner steals the episode for me. Nothing sums up Skinner's lack of cool better than his back and forth over buying a motorised tie-rack.

D: I don't know why but there's just something about Homer in a muumuu that makes me so happy, especially when you throw in his fat guy hat. What he does in 'King Size Homer' is something we'd all love to do but know we shouldn't: overindulge in some of life's tastiest treats, be it fried chicken or play dough.

M: Oh, if only. It's pretty much how I envision people who work from home live their lives, by the way. Not necessarily the obesity, but definitely the trying out of fabric softener samples.

'Lisa the Vegetarian'
(Season 7, Episode 5)
Review by Dando

After the family visit a petting zoo, Lisa becomes so attached to a lamb that she decides she can no longer bring herself to eat meat. This causes a fracture at home, as Homer is planning a big BBQ. Lisa's decision is met with ridicule by all, and her fury results in her sabotaging the BBQ. Ultimately, special guest stars Paul and Linda McCartney teach her how to accept the choices of others.

For many, 'Lisa the Vegetarian' is remembered for giving people a reason to sing about salad. For the rest of us, it's an episode that shaped the way in which we live our lives.

Not only did it introduce the idea of vegetarianism to a whole new generation of youth, a concept rarely tackled in a television comedy, let alone a cartoon, but it also promoted the underlying theme of tolerance and acceptance of opposing beliefs. A lesson that has only become more relevant in a post social media world.

Lisa is stuck in a world where very little makes sense to her. Her ideologies are often met with patronising laughter and ridicule, such as her attempt to offer guests a fresh batch of gazpacho (tomato soup served ice cold) at Homer's BBBQ. Her excitement in showing every-body an alternative to meat quickly becomes an embarrassing moment for both Lisa and Homer. Homer's unjustified over-the-top reaction to Lisa's dish drives a wedge between the two.

From the beginning of the series it's established that Lisa and Homer are opposites in almost every feasible way. Intelligence, morals, beliefs, the lot. However, the one similarity they share is an unbridled father–daughter connection, a connection that reigns supreme here with a little help from 'a piggy-ba . . . a veggie-back ride.'

The beauty of this episode is that it's not written as a biased commercial for vegetarianism. David S. Cohen could've very easily positioned Lisa as a hero for choosing to say no to meat, leaving everyone else as the carnivorous villains. Alternatively, it would have been easy to paint Lisa as a veggie-terrorist trying to disrupt the normal order. Instead, focus is placed on an uneducated father who simply doesn't understand why his little girl suddenly hates him for what he has always eaten. Homer and Lisa both learn a valuable lesson here: Homer must accept that being a vegetarian is a mindset and not just a choice, whereas Lisa must stop unfairly judging and forcing her beliefs upon everybody else.

It isn't until Lisa stumbles across Apu in his secret garden with Paul and Linda McCartney that she fully grasps the negligence of her actions in stealing the pig from Homer's BBBQ. By revealing themselves to be vegans, they show Lisa the importance of tolerance. Lisa quickly flips from being a holier-than-thou do-gooder to feeling like a terrible person in their eyes for so much as drinking milk. It shows Lisa the other side of prejudice and acceptance. It couldn't have been written more perfectly.

This was the story that made me view *The Simpsons* from a whole new perspective. No longer did I relate to the rebellious antics of Bart, for it was now evidently clear that I was in fact Lisa all along. That was a strange realisation to reach as a 9-year-old boy, but one I've come to understand with time. Her passion for animals is something I share, and although this episode may not have left me a vegetarian, I've never eaten lamb since.

Perhaps the most important element of 'Lisa the Vegetarian' is that it wasn't just a one-and-done. In a show where characters don't age and things return to normal each week, this was an iconic shift in the characters' timeline that changed the show's direction forever. Had Lisa once again hopped aboard the carnivorous bandwagon in future seasons, it would have undermined everything this episode taught us. Kudos must be given to Paul and Linda, who only agreed to guest star if Lisa remained a vegetarian for the duration of the series. Twenty-two years and almost 500 episodes later, Lisa has become a global symbol of vegetarianism that transcends the show itself.

In hindsight, it's quite astonishing to think that, for 132 episodes, Lisa Simpson was a fully fledged meat eater. Her vegetarianism is now so instilled in her character that whenever I watch a rerun showing Lisa gorging on Marge's world-famous pork chops, my immediate thought is that it must be a continuity error. However, the fact that we unknowingly followed Lisa on a six-year journey only added to the impact of her eventual decision to say goodbye to meat. Vegetarianism was instantly so true to who she was that it makes you wonder why it wasn't discovered sooner.

Breaking down many barriers, 'Lisa the Vegetarian' influenced my thought-process and behaviour more than any other episode in the series' history, teaching me that an opposing belief is not necessarily an incorrect one. While it may have aired more than two decades ago, its themes remain a valuable lesson for anybody lucky enough to have watched it.

What did we learn?

You don't win friends with salad.

'Marge Be Not Proud'
(Season 7, Episode 11)
Review by Mitch

After Marge tells Bart she will be unable to get him a copy of a new video game for Christmas, Bart gets caught attempting to shoplift it from the local Try-N-Save. Out in the cold having lost his mother's trust, Bart tries to set things right.

It has been written by others that 'Marge Be Not Proud' suffers for falling into the television trope commonly referred to as the 'Very Special Episode'. The term refers to when a generally light-hearted TV show tackles a serious subject, usually promoted with a phrase such as 'Tonight, on a very special episode of . . .' Often, these episodes would introduce or use an external character, for example Tom Hanks playing a drunk uncle in *Family Ties*.

In my opinion, this is not one of those episodes. In having Bart commit the crime, we have an established troublemaker learning a lesson. It feels wholly natural and earned by the seasons that have come before it. Given that we are dealing with a mother and her son, there's virtually no way for the episode not to be sentimental, nor is there any reason for it not to be. It strikes a balance between lessons and laughs, the latter primarily

235

coming from Homer, who is reduced to comic relief in what is the best Bart/Marge story ever seen.

It gets off to a slow start with the Krusty Christmas Special being the weakest element of the episode. The scene exists to set up the first Christmas episode since 'Simpsons Roasting on an Open Fire' and while it doesn't hit the mark comedically, it does set the scene well. It reminded me of watching Letterman on Christmas Eve, or the excellent *Very Murray Christmas* more recently. The commercial for Bonestorm, in which a muscle-bound Santa crashes through a wall, picks things up instantly. The commercial sneaks in a great take on video games and marketing: The 'boring' game the kids are playing is a fighting game in which a man is literally fist-fighting a tank. Bonestorm is ... essentially the same thing: two guys closely resembling Mortal Kombat's Goro fist-fighting set to heavy-metal. To my parents, every brawler I played probably looked identical, too. To be fair, as much as I love Uncharted and Zelda, there's a primal desire in a lot of us that a game like Bonestorm appeals to, eyerolls be damned.

As Bart is set on a collision course with his destiny, a few elements are established that pay off later in the episode. Chief among them is the class struggle that plays into Bart's sense of injustice at not being able to obtain a copy. In being unable to afford the game, Bart takes the role of the underdog. Marge's purity and love for her family is also underscored early on. She doesn't long for presents for Christmas, all she wants is just one good photo of the family. Just one photo that Bart hasn't ruined. Marge rarely shows signs of character development, but this really speaks to the core of who she is and how she sees the world. It makes the later betrayal of trust all the more powerful.

The class struggle is enhanced when Bart is at the Try-N-Save and sees a spoiled kid getting whatever he wants, including two copies of Bonestorm. That, coupled with peer pressure, is enough to push Bart over the edge. Crucially, he retains an element of guilt in his actions, again allowing us to stay sympathetic towards him. Bart isn't doing this to be bad, he's only doing it because he really wants something and has no other possible way to get it. Now, take my word for it, that line will *not* hold up in court, but it does hold up enough to have us feel at least a little bit sorry for Bart.

The escape sequence showcases some of the show's best direction. It may not be *Ocean's Eleven* in terms of caper, but the tension is palpable as Bart makes his exit, only for the hand of a security guard (the always intimidating Lawrence Tierney) to clamp down on his shoulder. While Bart initially avoids punishment, his relief is short-lived when he finds out that the family Christmas photo will be taken back at the Try-N-Save. Again, the direction is superb as Bart tries to avoid security in the store, only to be caught at the perfect time to ruin another family photo. The fact that the Simpsons still got the photo framed to take home is also (a) hilarious and (b) a set-up for the final denouement.

When Marge discovers Bart has shoplifted, we get an excellent exhibition of pathos. Mike Scully drew on his own memories of shoplifting as a child during the writing, and he conveys a great sense of fear and shame on the part of Bart. It's not Homer yelling at him that upsets him the most, it's Marge not saying anything at all. The feeling of disappointing her is worse than the feeling of angering her could ever be. Bart is lost without his mother's love. The time spent dwelling on his emptiness, and on Marge's cold shoulder, sets the scene for a wonderful redemption that hits all of the right notes.

'Marge Be Not Proud' is a throwback to older episodes of *The Simpsons*. Like some of the best early episodes, it finds a balance between sentimentality and comedy in a way that few other shows can. It also has its share of iconic moments: it gave birth to the name of our podcast, it gave us Thrillho, and it gave us Lee Carvallo's Putting Challenge. That all adds up to a very special episode, indeed.

What did we learn?

Fads come, and fads go, but the cup-and-ball will last forever.

Season 8 (1996-97)
In Conversation

DANDO: Much like Season 7, it's very hard to pick fault with anything from Season 8. From the Emmy-Award-winning 'Homer's Phobia' to the outstanding musical numbers of 'Simpsoncalifragilisticexpiala(Annoyed Grunt)cious', this season is filled with so many moments that prove the writing team were still in their creative prime.

MITCH: It's really a great continuation of Bill Oakley and Josh Weinstein's desire to keep the show connected to its heritage while trying to explore new ground. From 'You Only Move Twice' where an entire new town was designed, to 'Mountain of Madness', where most of the episode takes place inside a cabin, there are a *lot* of episodes that didn't feel like typical *Simpsons*, but also feel perfectly at one with the rest of the show.

D: My two favourite examples of that are 'The Springfield Files' and 'The Simpsons Spin-Off Showcase'. The showcase basically has a 'Treehouse of Horror' structure, just without the horror. These short stories always have me crying with laughter.

M: I love the way that each segment has a unique feel that perfectly captures the style of show that it's riffing on. 'The Love-Matic Grampa', for example, almost feels like a show that could have existed in the 60s, airing alongside *My Mother the Car*. They made sure to stay faithful to the way those sitcoms used to be shot,

239

emulating a three-camera approach. It's that attention to detail that I've always loved about the show.

D: This formula could have easily become an annual tradition, offering the writers a fresh palette of ideas to explore with some of the show's most beloved secondary characters. It has a 'so bad that it's good' vibe that makes sure you never take it too seriously. Still, I'd give anything to see more of Wiggum and Skinner as a crime fighting duo trying to take down Big Daddy on a weekly basis.

M: The idea was that if they deliberately wrote outlandish ideas for spin-offs it would become a comment on their views of the quality of spin-offs in general. While it's true that great spin-offs are few and far between, it's still ironic, given that *The Simpsons* itself was a spin-off from the Tracey Ullman shorts.

D: Some of the series' most memorable one-time characters are featured here: Rex Banner, Larry Burns, Frank Grimes – even everyone's favourite supervillain Hank Scorpio. While they may have only been on our screens for less than 20 minutes, these characters all left behind an incredible legacy of their own.

M: Well, Larry Burns is essentially Rodney Dangerfield being Rodney Dangerfield, and is all the better for it. If there's anything more enjoyable than 20 minutes of one-liners from the king of one-liners, I'm yet to come across it. He gets all the respect in the world from me.

D: '*El Viaje Misterioso de Nuestro Jomer*' . . .

M: I'm sorry, what?

D: 'The Mysterious Voyage of Our Homer' . . .

M: Ah.

D: . . . is an episode that never translated well with me as a kid, I just didn't get it. Even now I still think Homer's

240

hallucination is more of an animation showcase than actual storytelling, but at least now I can appreciate the genius of it.

M: It's one I've always been in two camps about. As you say, I can totally appreciate the brilliance of the animation, but it comes at the expense of story, and doesn't quite hit the mark in terms of visual metaphor either. It's probably best enjoyed as a piece of artwork, although the chilli cook-off opening act is excellent. I love how strongly Springfieldians will get behind a fair.

D: What's interesting is that George Meyer pitched this idea during the third season, which due to technological restrictions probably would have resulted in a very different episode. You can just imagine how excited David Silverman must have been when he heard Oakley and Weinstein had decided to resurrect the idea for this season. Being the perfectionist that he is, Silverman animated the hallucination sequence almost entirely on his own to ensure it turned out just how he had envisioned.

M: It would be interesting to see just how much more could have been done if it had been made after the switch to digital. It could have opened the door to some smooth sweeping camera angles that could have perhaps heightened the sensory experience. Part of me would love to see their next movie be a *Fantasia*-style experience full of hallucination.

D: The episode also features one of the most underrated guest appearances of all time, Johnny Cash as the Space Coyote. I've always loved the idea that Johnny Cash was chewing on his own sleeve when recording the scene with the coyote gnawing on Homer's leg.

M: I'd throw in Frank Ormond from 'The Twisted World of Marge Simpson' as a challenger to that title. He may not have the enduring quotability, but I guess I'm just a sucker for Jack Lemmon. He's my favourite kind of guest star, somebody who isn't a household name, therefore hasn't been brought in purely for a ratings spike, but somebody who the producers clearly wanted to work with. Those sorts of stars tend to give the greatest performances, usually because they are truly great performers to begin with.

D: If you were a fan of both *The Simpsons* and *Frasier* in the 90s then 'Brother from Another Series' was everything you could've hoped for. There's so much of Frasier Crane in Sideshow Bob that it was only fitting that David Hyde Pierce should play his brother Cecil. It's essentially a crossover, with an abundance of *Frasier* references that will make any fan smile. From the use of the *Frasier* theme to Cecil mistaking Bart for Maris, this episode is just so much fun.

M: They even go as far as using a *Frasier*-style title card leading into Cecil's apartment. David Hyde Pierce slots in perfectly, I love his defence of the four years he spent at clown college . . .

D: 'I'll thank you not to refer to Princeton that way.'

M: We also get an origin story of Bob. It had always been odd that somebody as dignified as Bob would lower himself to the role of clown-sidekick, but as we see, it was actually Cecil who had the dream of being a clown. Bob's quiet humiliation as his hair explodes outward after being hit by a pie is a brilliant marriage of acting and animation.

D: It's probably my favourite incarnation of Bob as he genuinely tries to do good by everybody he's ever burned in the past, even going as far as risking his own life in order to save Bart. To be honest, it's always bothered me that Bart and Lisa never stood up for Bob when

Wiggum was arresting him without any evidence of foul play on his behalf.

M: To be fair, Lisa does try, but she runs into the brick wall that is Chief Wiggum's incompetence. Even a voluntary confession from Cecil isn't enough to swing him around to seeing Bob as innocent.

D: You and I are both dog lovers. How do you feel about 'The Canine Mutiny'?

M: Of all the things Bart has ever done – cutting the head off the statue of Jebediah, shoplifting, graffitiing the town, playing with Mrs. Krabappel's emotions – giving away Santa's Little Helper is the one that I cannot possibly forgive him for. Of course, he quickly realises his mistake and the pair manage to get reunited and take down a drug dealer in the process, but still. You just don't do that.

D: I must admit I've discovered a new-found love for 'Simpsoncalifragilisticexpiala(Annoyed Grunt)cious' ever since we were lucky enough to interview the voice of Shary Bobbins, Maggie Roswell. Every time I watch it I'm taken back to the moment she sang 'Cut Every Corner' for us live in person. That was seriously one of those surreal moments that make me realise how giving and kind the actors on the show can be.

M: 'Homer vs. the 18th Amendment' is a great example of an episode I've grown to love more over time. I mean, when I was younger I still found it funny on a basic level, but as I've grown up and watched movies like *The Untouchables*, or even shows like *Boardwalk Empire*, you realise what a great take on prohibition this episode provides. And, of course, Rex Banner is the most intense take on an Eliot Ness imaginable, punching through glass to interrogate Barney. The man would stop at nothing to uphold the law.

D: It also gave us some of Homer's best ever life advice regarding beer . . .

M: The cause of . . .

D: And solution to . . .

M&D: All of life's problems.

High five, fade to black.

'Homer's Enemy'
(Season 8, Episode 23)
Review by Dando

After seeing a human-interest story about a man named Frank Grimes, Mr. Burns is so touched that he immediately hires him as Executive Vice-President. However, the following day, Burns appoints a dog instead after seeing a similar story, bumping Grimes to work with Homer. Seeing Homer's behaviour and subsequent lack of consequence up-close proves too much for Grimes to handle, and he ultimately snaps in a fit of rage, grabbing high-voltage cables that result in an instant death.

Dark in subject matter and sparse on light-gags, 'Homer's Enemy' is an episode that continues to divide the series' fanbase. It introduced us to one of the most 'normal' characters in Frank Grimes, a man who has had to work hard every day of his life, which in return has actually given him quite little. As a result, he's understandably bitter, cold and socially wooden, making him the perfect foil for our beloved idiot, Homer.

I've never been a fan of Frank Grimes as a person, yet I admire everything that he represents as a character. I often compare him to Superintendent Chalmers, in that neither of them *feel* like Simpsons characters. They're more a representation of what would happen if some-body from the real world entered the insane bubble of Springfield. As viewers we never question the behaviour of the characters in the show, since we see it simply as that: a television show. Grimes on the other hand was someone who had to try and process this insanity as reality.

Basing his performance on William H. Macy, Azaria has said that this role was the most difficult in both execution and preparation. Being a cast member from the show's inception, Azaria was able to understand and channel the frustration of Grimes like no other, success-fully transforming this hard-working American hero into an antagonist of sorts as he becomes fixated on wanting everyone else to hate Homer as much as he does.

If this were any other show, we as an audience would feel nothing but sympathy for the down-trodden Grimes. He's lived through more hardship and pain in his short life than any of us could even begin to imagine. Yet writer John Swartzwelder manages to make us point and laugh as fan-favourite Homer's obnoxious behav-iour continues to drive him to the point of insanity, such as eating Grimes' special diabetic lunch, or using his personalised pencils to clean his ears.

Grimes challenged fans to view Homer from an unbi-ased perspective. We all loved Homer despite his obvious flaws, but was he as terrible as Grimes believed him to be? There's an argument for and against. Homer's behaviour was irritatingly baffling throughout the epi-sode, yet just like us, his friends and family had learned to accept it as part of the package, for we know that deep down he is a kind-hearted soul who would do anything for his loved ones. Grimes on the other hand never got the opportunity to meet and understand the real Homer, nor did he want to. Of course, Homer is so incompetent at, well, life in general, that it's easy to understand why someone with Grimes' background would feel such disdain for him. Despite his work ethic, Grimes can never catch a break, whereas Homer is never truly held accountable for his actions.

As much as Grimes is Homer's harshest critic, 'Homer's Enemy' as a whole is an episode that the writers and showrunners use to self-critique their own work. Admittedly, I was not a huge fan of the episode when it first aired, it just felt unnecessarily pessimistic as it highlights reasons why we should hate Homer and how in a fair and just world he doesn't deserve to have a beautiful home and family, let alone lobster for dinner. However, over time I've learned to appreciate the self-deprecating commentary that came with all of Grimes' finger-pointing, coming to see it as a statement from the writing staff that they were well aware of the absurdity of the characters they had created . . .

Most of those who dislike 'Homer's Enemy' aren't fans of its unique tone, including former showrunner Mike Reiss, who claims that it's in 'bad taste'. It can't be denied that it spends a lot more time focusing on gallows humour than we've come to expect; however, it's impossible not to give kudos to the likes of Swartzwelder, Oakley and Weinstein for wanting to challenge themselves. The show produces some of its best work when it refuses to stick to the formula ('22 Short Films About Springfield', 'Trilogy of Error', '24 Minutes', etc.) and 'Homer's Enemy' is certainly no exception.

What did we learn?

Frank Grimes is most certainly not Homer Simpson.

An Interview with Rob Oliver

Rob Oliver has worked in virtually every role possible in the animation department on The Simpsons, *from character artist all the way through to directing episodes. He first came to the show in Season 8, and has gone on to direct some of the most critically acclaimed episodes of the last decade. Here, he speaks to us about his journey on the show and his early mentors, as well as the need to keep pushing forward and to strive for perfection at all times.*

You started working for the show in Season 8. What was your first memory of seeing The Simpsons *prior* **to then? Was it always something you'd wanted to work on?**

Yes, I was hired in Season 8, in 1996. I was 19 years old. It was my first job ever. I remember watching *The Tracey Ullman Show* with my brothers, in Michigan; and I also remember when *The Simpsons* became a show. We watched it religiously. We loved it, it was hilarious! And I never, ever, ever, ever, ever dreamed that I could work on the show. I mean, I was a kid in Michigan. And even though I always saw those names flash by in the credits, not once did I stop to think about how it was made or who made it. When I thought about jobs in animation, I thought about Disney (who didn't?); and Disney was simply unattainable. So, to me, the fact that I ever got a job on *The Simpsons*, and that I have lasted this long on it, is surreal.

You have had a long career on The Simpsons *in many different roles. Was directing always the end goal, or did it just evolve that way?*
My career definitely evolved into what it is. It's all been completely unplanned. When I was hired as a character layout artist, I knew nothing about animation. I knew how to draw, I knew how to listen and learn, and I knew how to put my head down and work hard. In the beginning of my time on *The Simpsons*, I would work feverishly on a scene and then run (yes, run!) the scene across the floor to my director's office. My cousin's husband, Tim Bailey (also a *Simpsons* director!) knew way more about animation and drew backgrounds on the show. He taught me what I needed to know to get on my feet . . . and then he kicked my butt whenever it needed kicking.

On each episode, and in each role on *The Simpsons*, I have continued to want to do more and more, and to have more and more input. As a character artist, I would draw maybe 20 or 40 scenes in an episode. And while animating the characters is a *lot* of fun (there is absolutely nothing like creating a funny piece of movement for these characters!), eventually I wanted the chance to have a more global view of each episode. I became restless and bored. Therefore, I moved into Assistant Directing and Storyboarding.

That move must have given you a great opportunity to develop skills for directing?

As a storyboard artist, I worked under two different supervising directors: Mark Kirkland and Mike B. Anderson. And as an assistant director, I learned mainly under three directors: David Silverman, Michael Polcino, and Mike Marcantel. But there have also been many other directors I've learned from: Steve Moore, Nancy Kruse, Pete Michels, Bob Anderson, Lance Kramer, Raymond Persi, Jim Reardon, and Matthew Nastuk, to name just a few. Working under, and with, so many talented artists and directors, I've learned great ways of how to tell a story; but I've also learned how to manage the pieces that go into the creation of that story.

What skills do you think best help you when you are directing an episode?
I love to work with artists and with creative minds, and to draw out of them what I can. And I also love to teach. Because of all these things, I relished the move to directing. It's more collaborative – working not just on a group of scenes for one director, but with all the writers, producers and designers; and all the storyboard, character, background, colour, FX, and CG artists. And it's that collaboration that I truly love!

How do you control the stress of such a high-pressure job?
I have a lot of fun as a director. It's a fun, fun job. And I like to share that fun with my crew. Therefore, I have three rules on all my episodes (posted in my office and at my artists' desks):
  1. Visit me at least once each day.
  2. Draw something funny each day.
  3. Have fun!

251

How do you maintain a dynasty from the inside? Do you draw influence from what worked in the past, or do you look to evolve and find what will work in the future?
I'm always looking at the old stuff. I love to watch and rewatch classic moments and episodes, so that I can make sure I'm still in touch with what the show was in the beginning. That being said, I love to push the boundaries and make each episode what I think it needs to be. I have relished the chance to do many special things with the look and art of this show. I think we always must evolve, while keeping a foot firmly rooted in the original style of the show.

Can you give us some examples of that evolution?
In 'Barthood', we pushed for incredibly long scenes, reminiscent of those in *Boyhood*. I used After Effects to add airborne dust particles to show how old and dusty and closed-up Grampa's garage is. I also storyboarded the first act, adding in influence and artwork from my sons – my son Brandon helped me draw the mural on the kitchen walls; and when Bart is on the living-room floor playing with cars, he is in an identical pose to how both of my boys – Brandon and Jared – played with their cars.

In 'Sky Police', we figured out a fantastic effect for Chief Wiggum's jetpack: we hand-animated a few faint white lines to show motion and thrust, and then we added in a computerised displacement behind those lines in order to show the air being forced out of the jetpack.

'Holidays of Future Passed' was set 30 years in the future; I made it a bleak, junky, grey world. The coolest part of that episode, I think, is the Ultranet – Lisa attaches a cord to a port in her neck and enters an internet, where she sees multitudes of people flying in and out of doors that represent different websites. That took a lot of work!

In 'Treehouse of Horror XXIV', I created a Seussian world for 'Oh, the Places You'll D'oh' (with Homer as the Fat in the Hat). I storyboarded it, which was a lot of fun, because I got to do a lot of things such as curving the backgrounds and adding hatch marks, and . . . well, just pushing the boundaries all around.

Also in 'Treehouse of Horror XXIV', we used an almost-sepia-tone colour scheme for *Freaks, No Geeks* (based on the 1932 movie *Freaks*). For framing the shots in this act, I used a lot of dark shadows, which movies in the black-and-white era did a lot. It turned out so beautiful!

In 'Puffless', we animated an army of animals and dressed the set in a more Disneyesque fashion, using highly detailed backgrounds and soft filters. I timed out the animals' actions to musical cues (à la Bambi, Pinocchio, etc.) instead of to dialogue, which was a fun thing to do! There are small moments and there are big battles, and they all work well with the music.

In 'Blazed and Confused', we used an amazing night-time colour scheme to mimic the glow-in-the-dark accessories worn at the desert festival we called Blazing Guy: we desaturated the colours for the characters and pumped up the brightness for all the glowing elements. It really stands out! The night-time visuals blow me away every time I watch it!

Finally, for 'The Town', in order to accurately represent the city of Boston, we utilised street-view maps. We were able to place the viewer at Faneuil Hall in the heart of Boston. Also in that episode, my assistant director Eddie Rosas storyboarded a great homage to Terry

Gilliam (of *Monty Python* fame). It's a fun mixture of real-looking buildings and the *Simpsons* style.

If you reflect on your journey, what are the biggest changes in the show during your time, besides the switch to digital? Besides the switch from drawing on paper to drawing on a Cintiq screen (still hand-drawn, mind you!), the biggest change was probably the change in the aspect ratio.

I think in 2009 or so, we switched from a 4:3 screen ratio (old television screen) to a 16:9 ratio (modern widescreen, HD). The different screen dimensions meant we had to start composing scenes completely differently. It's a much more horizontally stretched frame, which lends itself to big, epic, sweeping, cinematic shots. In our character- and joke-driven animated sitcom, the wide screen makes it tougher to show a medium shot on a character without having a lot of empty screen on the sides. Matt Groening is always pushing us to be more cinematic, and to use the entire wide screen, and it took a lot of getting used to, but now when we try to go backward and compose to a squarer format it feels very restricting!

You essentially got to direct a Frasier *reunion in your second episode, 'Funeral for a Fiend'. Were you a fan of the show? How was it, getting to play with those actors?* I wasn't necessarily a big fan of *Frasier*, but I'm really, really fortunate to have been able to direct that episode. *Frasier* was a giant of a show, and the actors and characters were all amazing and memorable. Sideshow Bob is an outstanding character alone, but add in the other two and you've got gold! In 'Funeral for a Fiend', each actor brought such fantastic reads, which made it much

more fun to animate. I love the mannerisms my character artists used for each character. The voices and the
designs and the acting all blended so well!

I don't know how it was ultimately recorded, but I can
just imagine all three actors (Kelsey Grammer, David
Hyde Pierce and John Mahoney) in the booth, recording
together, and really making it a reunion! I can also
imagine myself there, soaking in all that talent!

**If stage is an actor's medium, film is a director's medium,
and TV is a writer's medium, what is animation?**
All of those *plus* an artist's medium.

ACTING: I pride myself on the acting I coax from my
artists. It is imperative that the acting for these characters
is natural and expressive. Often, I will have an artist personally act out for me the acting they're trying to draw. If
they can't do it, we keep at it until it's what we need. I
spend half my day acting out lines of dialogue!

DIRECTING: I pay an enormous amount of attention to the cinematic qualities of my singular shots and
my storytelling and how I'm leading the viewer (even
subconsciously) through the story. I'm always talking
about what an element of a scene or sequence does subconsciously to or for the viewer, and I'm sure it annoys
the hell out of my team.

WRITING: Our writers do a darn fine job.

DRAWING: What is animation without the proper
visuals? It all requires many things to be right: proper emotion, proper timing, proper composition . . . etc., etc., etc.

**You received an Emmy nomination for 'Holidays of
Future Passed', and you revisited characters at an older**

age in 'Barthood'. Is this coincidence, or would you like more opportunities to explore The Simpsons *outside of their age-bubble?*

I think it is purely a coincidence. The writers don't look at me and say, 'Now there's a fella that can draw older people.' (At least I hope they don't.) In both episodes, it was a real challenge to design the characters as they progressed through their lives. I was very hands-on in the design of the characters in both cases, and I am proud that we created some older versions of these characters that are still quite appealing.

One enormous difficulty in 'Holidays' was that we had to see a 30-year age progression via the family's Christmas cards. First, we perfected our ending designs, and then we had to fill in all the different ages in between – tweaking, tweaking, and tweaking some more. That sequence took a looooong time to finish!

Were you expecting the media coverage around Smithers coming out in 'The Burns Cage', or did it take you by surprise?

I did not expect it at all. We've always known that Smithers is gay, so it never crossed my mind that we were creating a big moment. The song that Smithers sings in the power plant was fun to do. We tried to really play up the loneliness that Smithers felt – and I think we got some really interesting shots in there, too!

What excites you more: a blank piece of paper, a storyboard, or a finished product?

I love every step of the process! Being a perfectionist and an artist, I like to have my hand in all of it.

Season 9 (1997-98)
In Conversation

DANDO: I can remember this being the time when a good portion of my friends were suddenly no longer interested in the show as much as I was. That's not so much a reflection on the quality of the writing, but more a case of my friends 'growing out' of watching it as they entered their teenage years.

MITCH: I was probably in that boat. I'm not sure that it was necessarily a purposeful thing; if anything, I think it was just that by now there were eight years' worth of episodes to rerun each night, so the newer episodes started to get a little bit lost in the wash. The show was a money-making machine, to the point that it felt like you couldn't watch a TV for more than two hours without an episode coming on, so it just solidified those first eight seasons as being so firmly etched in my brain.

D: When you go back and look through the episodes, it becomes so noticeable just how jarring the show became this season. With so many new and old writers contributing, it created such a blend of styles all fighting to showcase their preferred direction for the show. In the one season, you get 'Lisa's Sax'; a heartfelt family-driven story, 'Natural Born Kissers'; an episode targeted towards an older audience and then there's 'The Principal and the Pauper', which divided fans and show members alike with its continuity-breaking story.

M: There was a subtle shift in writing style where the jokes in parts seemed a little bit more telegraphed. Having watched a lot of the show by now, I was starting to identify lines that were clearly just there to set up for a punchline, which robbed it of its impact. As I say, it was only small, but a character like Bart in certain episodes felt like he existed only for a comic-relief quip that never really advanced anything. Overall, I still find these episodes very funny, but I could sense a formula creeping in.

D: It's no secret that 'Principal and the Pauper' was met with a barrage of criticism from the media and fans alike. The way it took a character we'd invested more than eight years of our life in and turned him into a fraud for the sake of a quick gag never sat well with me either. I often give credit to Oakley and Weinstein for their innovation in going against the grain with episodes like '22 Short Films About Springfield' and 'The Simpsons Spin-Off Showcase', but this was an experiment that probably should have never happened. In saying that, Martin Sheen's performance as the real Seymour Skinner was most certainly a high point of the season.

M: This is a point that you and I differ on. I never had a problem with it at the time, and once I'd learned of the criticism I went back and watched it, trying to look for issues, but I feel like it was handled well for two reasons. For one thing, the episode ending serves to reset the continuity with the whole town agreeing to collectively wash their memories and return to normal. Secondly, in my eyes it doesn't *change* any aspect of Skinner's backstory, it just adds a new layer. He met the real Skinner in Vietnam, so his flashbacks could well have been him, throw in an element of the unreliable narrator whenever Armin/Skinner is telling a war story, and this doesn't actually break anything. Crucially, it's also one of the funniest episodes from the season.

D: 'Bart Star' is an episode I tend to lump into the same category as all the underdog sporting films I grew up watching in the 90s like *The Mighty Ducks* and *Little Giants*, where a bunch of misfits find a way to take home the championship. It's filled with cliché but that doesn't detract from the fun.

M: Well, importantly, it's filled with the *right* clichés. There's a reason those movies follow little battlers up against a stronger team. It's brain-candy for us. I also love a good trick-play to win a big game, and Nelson using Bart as a battering ram to run the field is up there with the best of them.

D: I've always loved watching Homer's armchair coaching before Flanders hands him the reins to the team, it reminds me of myself when I'm watching my beloved Geelong Cats play.

M: Everybody's an expert from the sidelines. And yes . . . there's a very much intended subtext about this book in that line.

D: Outside of 'Bart Star', we don't get too many Homer and Bart episodes this season, the only other one being 'Bart Carny' featuring a fantastic appearance from Jim Varney as Cooder. It's a shame because overall Homer and Bart's schemes are generally a whole lot of fun.

M: What we do get in place of that, though, is a greater mix of characters who don't normally interact spending time together. 'Das Bus', for example, has a group of the kids who wouldn't ever really be hanging out together, forced to spend time with each other on a deserted island. It's probably a by-product of looking for new story ideas, and a natural expansion of the *Simpsons* universe.

D: Or in 'The Joy of Sect', Groundskeeper Willie is one of the main resistance fighters alongside Reverend Lovejoy and Ned Flanders.

M: That's an episode that almost feels like a bit of a time capsule in comedy circles. There was a period in the 90s where cults were all the rage, with everything from *Seinfeld* to *Family Guy* taking potshots at the Heaven's Gate movement, but it doesn't seem to be as widespread any more. It's also one that sticks out in my memory on a weekly basis. I still think of 'leader beans' whenever I have baked beans for breakfast.

D: For a man who is self-proclaimed 'pro-gun', Swartzwelder managed to produce a really unbiased perspective on gun control in 'The Cartridge Family'. Sam Simon actually pitched a similar idea in the first few seasons, which I'm sure gun critics would have jumped all over.

M: Certainly, the way the first episode was pitched almost comes across as pro-gun propaganda, but it comes down to the delivery. The writers worked hard to come across as apolitical, not trying to force anybody into a conclusion of their own. It went over my head as a kid, my only take-out from this episode is that it was very clearly anti-soccer.

D: This season features one of my all-time favourite subplots: Apu creating the Freak-E-Mart after Jasper freezes himself in 'Lisa the Simpson'. You just have to love the lengths Apu will go to in order to make a quick buck, taking advantage of what he assumed was a dead guy in his freezer.

M: Well, you've gotta play the hand you're dealt in life. Jasper finally being thawed out is such a classic moment, as he walks off in awe of what he assumes to be the futuristic food, moon-pie, a product that dates back to 1917.

D: The key story is also fantastic as Lisa deals with the prospect of a deteriorating intelligence after being unable to solve a simple brain teaser at school. I'm not going to lie, I couldn't solve it either when I first watched it. The ending can feel a little bit like an easy-out, but it does contain my most quoted line from the season: 'I step in front of cars and sue the drivers.' When I was 16 I jokingly included that in my résumé when applying online for my first job, assuming I'd never get hired anyway. In a remarkable turn of events the office lady was a massive *Simpsons* fan and thought it was hilarious. Two weeks later I was serving meat in a deli.

M: I assume only to later be sued by somebody who deliberately dropped some cold cuts on the ground and then slipped on them?

D: I'm unable to comment on an ongoing investigation.

M: As I look through the episodes, I'm yet again finding myself connecting most with a Lisa episode, 'Lost our Lisa'. It's not so much the desire to visit a museum, but I have also had some horrible experiences catching buses in my youth. The very first time I tried to catch a bus to school, I ended up on a bus to a girls-only college. The bus was, not surprisingly, entirely filled with girls, which was *not* as awesome as movies like *Dumb and Dumber* would have you believe. It involved far fewer bikinis, and a red-faced me ultimately bailing out at a red-light after the driver saw my plight.

D: So, as somebody who didn't watch the season as much when you were younger, what do you think of it now?

M: I still view the season highly. If anything, it suffers only due to the success of what had come before it. While I don't think it was at its peak, it was still 90% of what it used to be, and better than anything else on TV at the time.

'Realty Bites'
(Season 9, Episode 9)
Review by Mitch

Tired of being cooped up in the house, Marge pushes for Homer to go out with her for some fun and adventure. A police auction wasn't exactly what she had in mind, and when Homer buys Snake's old car without discussing it, she is pushed further over the edge. Walking home alone, she comes across Lionel Hutz selling real estate, and decides to make a run at the profession herself.

May 27, 1998 is one of the first times I remember being consciously aware of the morning news as a child. My parents would often put the news on in the morning to stop cartoons distracting me while I was getting ready for school. But what I heard on that day stopped me in my tracks, for it was the day the world lost Phil Hartman. Just five months earlier, 'Realty Bites' went to air, and featured his final speaking role as Lionel Hutz.

It's hard to compare the very real loss of a human that colleagues and friends of Phil's would have felt on that day to the imagined loss of fictional characters, but I'll do it anyway. When you constantly create characters who are larger than life, those characters create lifelike emotions when they are lost. As fans grieved the world over, even at the age of 10 I knew that we were losing a once in a lifetime talent. One who courtesy of his continual appearances on *Saturday Night Live* and *The Simpsons* had influenced the comedic styling of many of my generation. From his first appearance as Hutz in 'Bart Gets Hit by A Car', through to taking over as Troy McClure, or his show-stealing effort as Lyle Lanley, Hartman created some of the most memorable characters in the show's history. We wanted to take a moment to just say thank you, and reflect on all the joy he brought to our lives.

It's fortuitous that what became his final speaking appearance would allow Hutz to shine in his new role as a real-estate agent. It's a perfect transition for Hutz as he switches from one hated profession to another. Ironically, despite being a terrible law-talkin'-guy, he comes across as a damn good realtor, teaching Marge the ropes of looking for the positives in a property: Small = Cozy; Dilapidated = Rustic; On Fire = Motivated Seller. The difference between the truth and *the truth* is one that I would later have to come to terms with as I was buying my own house for the first time. My friends described my cheap two-bedroom unit as a tiny cesspit where hope goes to die. I preferred to think of it as a snug collector of dreams. It's all in the detail.

I've always been a fan of fish-out-of-water scenarios in the *Simpsons* universe. Be it Marge as a police officer, Homer as a boxer, Bart as a gangster or Lisa in a beauty pageant, they always offer ways to see new jokes about our favourite characters. By thrusting Marge into a *Glengarry Glen Ross* style real estate agency, not only does writer Dan Greaney find a way to explore if honesty and sales can mix, he is also able to create several new characters. The sales agents are instantly quotable, be it Cookie Kwan defending her west side territory, or Nick Callahan introducing me to the word 'Boo-Yah.'

Of the new characters introduced here, one stands supreme. Trembling head and shoulders above the rest, and one of the few truly loved characters to be introduced so late in the series. I'm speaking, of course, of Gil Gunderson. Inspired by Jack Lemmon's *Glengarry* salesman, Shelley Levine, Gil quickly became a fan favourite, and writers' favourite. He would go on to reappear many times, often in a new job, always a failure, never losing optimism.

Homer's side-plot of purchasing Lil' Bandit from the police auction flits in and out of the episode, seemingly without purpose. It does exist to break up Marge's main scenes, and for comic relief. It includes one of my favourite cold openings of all time as Homer enjoys what he thinks is a lazy Saturday, only to be told it is in fact Wednesday. It's a sub-plot that creates a point of contention between myself and my wife, Ash, as she is insistent that I too once bought a car without telling her. I like to think that I simply acquired some surprise transportation. Again, it's all in the details.

What can't be argued is that the scenes with Lil' Bandit supply some of the zanier visual comedy the show has to offer. Homer driving the car on two wheels offers a taste of this. Snake and Homer later fighting on the hood of the car as it careens down the road offers a great over-the-top action scene that wouldn't be out of place in a Bond film, but it's the *Road Runner* style trap that results in Kirk Van Houten losing an arm that gets the biggest laugh.

These scenes appear to be happening in their own bubble, at first, but, in a brilliant final act, literally crash into the main plot as Homer and Snake destroy the one house Marge has been able to sell. It affords one final scene with Hutz, in a *Lethal Weapon* inspired moment chastising Marge as being a loose cannon but, above all else, for returning Ned's deposit cheque. As we say goodbye to Phil, Marge is fired and returns to her normal life. *The Simpsons*, however, would never be the same again.

What did we learn?

Real Estate agents get to live in a house until it's sold.

'Natural Born Kissers'
(Season 9, Episode 25)
Review by Dando

Homer and Marge find that their relationship is lacking spark in the bedroom, a fact not helped by their wedding anniversary plans being ruined. After a series of unfortunate events finds them taking shelter in a barn, they find that the fear of getting caught is just what they need to reignite their love-life. The escalation of their thrill leads to them needing to make their way home from Sir Putt-A-Lot's whilst completely nude.

'Natural Born Kissers' had one of the most unusual build-ups to any episode I can remember. Promoted as 'adults-only' and featuring numerous shots of Homer and Marge running around naked in the commercial, it sent my young mind into overdrive as I tried to imagine exactly what I'd be seeing. At the time I was only nine years old and the closest I'd come to 'adult' content was watching Pamela & Co. run around in wet swimsuits on *Baywatch*, so you can imagine my anticipation in the days leading up to it. In fact, I remember trying to ensure my mum didn't see the commercial herself, because I thought if she did, there'd be no way she'd let me watch it. What made it even more intriguing was that Channel

10 decided to air it at the special time of 9.30 p.m. Monday as opposed to the usual 7.30 p.m. Sunday, even teasing that due to its nature they might never air it again. While the episode may not be quite as raunchy as my imagination had envisioned, it's arguably the most effective and 'real' story we get based around Homer and Marge's marriage.

What *The Simpsons* has always done well is showcase Marge's natural desire for having sex with her husband. While the wives in most classic sitcoms were turned off by the thought of making love to their spouse, Marge is often the one suggesting that she and Homer 'rock the Casbah'. She is well aware that a healthy sex life is an important part of any marriage, so you can understand her concern when a surprise visit by Santa's Little Helper is the most exciting thing to happen in their bedroom on the night of her and Homer's 11th wedding anniversary. Castellaneta and Kavner shine in this scene, giving a true feeling of awkwardness as Homer and Marge attempt to kick off the proceedings. 'Homie you got your, your elbow in . . .' has always been one of my favourite lines from Marge.

There's no doubt that we definitely get more nudity in this episode than we'd grown accustomed to, which helped justify its late-night billing, especially since we get our first glimpse of Marge's bare behind. However, it is Homer's bare arse that steals the show here as it gets compared to a 'hefty bag of meat' when the townspeople reach into the windmill, then prevents a field goal from being completed, and gets dragged along the glass ceiling of a church in a scene that instantly created an unforgettable visual almost purpose-built for the episode's commercial. There's also something about a cow secretly perving on Marge and Homer doing it in a barn that never fails to get a laugh; in fact Groening has said it's his favourite lead-in to an ad break. Despite those moments all being fantastic in their own right, to me nothing beats the visual of Homer covering his nipples with teacups when the maid walks into their room at the Snuggler's Cove.

Aside from the nudity, the sexual context of the conversations are also far more blatant than usual. When sex is referenced on the show it's often done through innuendo, yet here writer Matt Selman didn't have the characters hold back. Homer's conversation with Lenny and Carl is about as close to real-life locker room talk as the show has ever delivered, particularly with Carl's confession that he'd assumed Marge would be a 'dynamo in the sack', only to completely switch gears when she arrives.

You can really tell that Selman was a true fan of the show by the way he includes subtle throwbacks to previous episodes, such as Homer finding the programme for Frank Grimes' funeral, or Homer and Marge returning to their old love-nest at Sir Putt-A-Lot's, even though this time it was the windmill and not the impregnable castle. The way Moe steals Helen Lovejoy's thunder by screaming 'Won't somebody please think of the children!' is also a nice touch that would please any diehard fan of the show. In saying all that, I can't help but feel a reference to Homer nibbling Marge's elbow was an obvious chance for a joke gone to waste.

The sub-plot to the episode involving Bart and Lisa's search for treasure with Grampa's metal detector served its purpose, keeping the kids preoccupied while Marge and Homer searched for new ways to keep their love flame burning. I've always been a fan of these simple side stories that take Bart and Lisa on a little adventure of their own. This one always reminds me of when my sister and I used a metal detector in our backyard: we didn't find any alternate endings to classic films but we did find one of my Street Sharks action figures that my sister forgot she'd buried in the sandpit.

While risqué in context, 'Natural Born Kissers' manages to keep itself well grounded with simplistic storytelling. Rather than abuse its adults-only classification with crude humour, it remains tasteful in how it explores a personal issue that I'm sure most married couples face over their journey together. Homer and Marge may be fictional characters in a cartoon, but their marriage is just as real as any other you'll ever see.

What did we learn?

Take a picture, it lasts longer.

'The Simpsons isn't good any more'
(Our Favourite Episodes
post-Season 12)

The title of this chapter is a comment that tends to get thrown around haphazardly these days, without any real thought or merit behind it. It's almost become an easy out for those who choose to remember only the show's earlier seasons, many of whom haven't even watched an episode in years. Is *The Simpsons* as consistently good as it was in 1995? Short answer, no. However, to simply dismiss the current crop of episodes purely based on the era in which they aired would be doing yourself an enormous disservice.

The common consensus is that the show's quality dipped somewhere between Seasons 10 and 12, which, I will admit, featured some rather questionable moments such as Swartzwelder's chaotic 'Kill the Alligator and Run'. That being said, sometimes you need to take the good with the bad – except in this case the good is actually quite great. 'Bart the Mother', 'Lisa Gets An "A"', 'Behind the Laughter', 'НОМЯ' and 'Trilogy of Error' are just a handful of my personal favourites from that era.

What we want to do here is shine a light on some of the quality episodes in recent seasons that deserve your appreciation. The episodes that prove that, even after 29 years, *The Simpsons* has still got it.

'The Seemingly Never-Ending Story'
(Season 17, Episode 13)

This story-within-a-story-within-a-story-within-a-story, known these days as the *Inception* method, about the hunt for hidden treasure gives us brilliant insights into how some of our most loved characters came to live in Springfield, including arguably my favourite Edna Krabappel moment of all time when she first meets Bart. It results in something that feels like a blend of flashback meets spin-off, as secondary characters like Snake and the Rich Texan take the spotlight. The writing is incredibly sharp as each story seamlessly intertwines with the next, leading to a fitting climax between some of Springfield's most notorious baddies.

Highlights: The origin of the name 'Jailbird', Burns spending some time with relatives

'24 Minutes'
(Season 18, Episode 21)

Much like 'The Springfield Files', the show delivers an incredibly funny crossover with another one of FOX's hit programmes at the time. The story follows Springfield Elementary's CTU (Counter Truancy Unit) attempt to prevent a stink bomb explosion at their annual bake sale, with the events taking place over the course of 20 minutes. It features all the trademarks of *24*; multiple split-screens, a timer before and after commercial breaks, as well as an unexpected plot twist that would make Jack and Chloe proud, both of whom also make guest cameos.

Highlights: The throwback to 'Bart the Genius', Homer and Milhouse's journey in Ol' Betsy.

'Eternal Moonshine of the Simpson Mind' (Season 19, Episode 9)

A Christmas episode with a twist, in that the only festive thing about it is the setting. In a take on 2004's *Eternal Sunshine of the Spotless Mind*, Homer must retrace his steps to learn why his family have seemingly abandoned him. It explores darker themes like fidelity, domestic violence and suicide, but still manages to leave you feeling all warm and fuzzy like any good holiday special.

Highlights: Duffman's secret shame, Homer's '39 Years in 50 seconds' time lapse video.

'The Debarted' (Season 19, Episode 13)

A spot-on parody of Martin Scorsese's Oscar-winning film that sees new kid Donny (voiced by Topher Grace) take on the role of DiCaprio as he is hired by Skinner to snitch on Bart. While it starts rather slowly, the writing excels in providing Donny with some great character depth that makes the episode's final scene so much more impactful. This truly is one of the great film parodies from the show, not quite on the level of 'Cape Feare', but enough references are thrown in to ensure it pleases any fans of *The Departed*, from the use of 'I'm Shipping Up to Boston' by the Dropkick Murphys in the chase sequence to ending the episode with a rat. It also gives us a fantastic Skinner/Chalmers moment that proves the Superintendent may just have a heart after all.

Highlights: Grace's performance, the table and cooler in Bart's treehouse, à la *That '70s Show*

'The Squirt and the Whale' (Season 21, Episode 19)

After a typical Homer scheme in the first act where he buys a wind turbine in order to save on electricity, the story shifts its focus to Bart and Lisa as they discover a beached whale. 'Bluella' is animated beautifully, drawn to look like a real-life whale as opposed to a Simpsonised version. You can see the fear and anguish in her eyes as the townpeople work together to help her in an act reminiscent of 'Radio Bart'. If you are an animal lover, it's easy to put yourself in Lisa's shoes as she dedicates herself to ensuring Bluella feels safe and comfortable as she lies helplessly on the shore. There's a moment midway through the episode that is as powerful as anything that's come before and is arguably one of the bravest moves in the show's history. If you have any form of a soul at all you'll be left crying like a baby just like I was.

Highlights: Homer's determination to do right by Lisa, Comic Book Guy's Shatner impersonation.

'Brick Like Me' (Season 25, Episode 20)

'It's not selling out, it's co-branding!' These are the first words we hear Homer say in this episode that sees Springfield transformed into Lego. While this could have very easily just resulted in a cheap gimmick that served nothing more than to get people talking, what we get is a genuinely heartfelt story between Homer and Lisa (of course) that adds a new dimension to their relationship that we've surprisingly never seen before. Visually this episode is stunning, particularly as iconic characters and locations are destroyed in classic Lego fashion and the writing proves that the staff are clearly fans of Lego themselves. While this may have taken over two years to produce, the end result is something everyone involved should certainly be proud of.

Highlights: Milhouse's Lego Bart, Homer's accidental racist taunt to Apu. (You'll understand.)

'Holidays of Future Passed'
(Season 23, Episode 9)

A flash-forward Christmas special set 30 years in the future where Bart is a divorced deadbeat father of two sons, Lisa is regretfully married to Milhouse, and they have a volatile teenage daughter, while Maggie is the most influential voice in music. This was going to be the series finale had FOX's contract dispute with the cast earlier that year not been resolved, which we'd honestly have been quite content with. This episode gives you a sense of closure as it gives an insight into how our favourite four-fingered family ended up. Everything's changed but it's still much the same, except Bart is now capable of having an adult conversation with his sister. Speaking of, their discussion in Bart's treehouse about parenthood is one of the show's finest moments in decades. A truly touching story that would've been a more than satisfying conclusion to the greatest television show of all time.

Highlights: Lisa's lesbian phase, The Benny Hilton, the new Chief Wiggum.

'Halloween of Horror'
(Season 27, Episode 4)

After years of Halloween specials, it's amazing that this is the first in-canon episode to revolve around Halloween itself. This wouldn't feel out of place in Season 9, with Homer at the core of the story, putting all that he believes in aside for the good of Lisa. When it turns into a home-invasion movie in the second act there is a legit-imate sense of fear that puts you on edge, allowing the comedy to be elevated as a form of relief. Visually, it's a delight, and a great example of how the digital format can be used to enhance a story.

Highlights: 'Grown-up Halloween', Lisa humming the theme from *Halloween* to calm herself, the best Hans Moleman joke since *Man Getting Hit by Football*.

'Barthood'
(Season 27, Episode 9)

A take on Richard Linklater's 2014 coming-of-age film *Boyhood*, this episode isn't your typical *Simpsons* par-ody. Usually the *Simpsons* staff tend to put their own wacky spin on a film's premise; however, writer Dan Greaney chooses to keep things more grounded here as we follow Bart over a 20-year journey starting at the age of six. It's hard to decide whether to accept this episode as canonical due to its format, but nevertheless it gives us a great insight into Bart's struggle to find his purpose as he deals with living in the shadows of his more intellec-tual and successful sister. While Future Bart is normally portrayed as a self-absorbed loser, 'Barthood' proves that there's more to this little hellraiser than his friends and family give him credit for.

Highlights: Grampa teaching Bart to drive, Wiggum realising he can't fly, the ending.

If there's one thing that we've learned in the process of writing this book, it's that the *Simpsons* staff are some of the most passionate, humble and giving people we've ever met. They continue to try and push this phenomenal show's legacy further into the future, adapting it for a new audience as it comes along.

The examples we've highlighted serve as reasons why we should *all* be hoping that the show continues running for many years to come. If it does, it's a certainty that we will get more great moments along the way.

If we lost this amazing part of our lives, it would be like losing a distant family member. One you saw all the time when you were younger, and even though you've since grown apart, there's a certain comfort in knowing they are still a part of the world, still making people smile, and while that's happening, there's still a chance that one day you will be able to reconnect.

We think that everybody needs a little bit of that feeling in their lives.

Long live *The Simpsons*.

Dando and Mitch.

Acknowledgements

Thank you to the following people, without whom this book would not have been possible: Nikki Isordia, Harry Shearer, Maggie Roswell, Joe Mantegna, Matt Schofield, Bill Oakley, Liz Climo, Mike B. Anderson, Rob Oliver, David Silverman, Huw Armstrong and the team at Penguin Random House.

We'd also like to extend a special thanks to all those who have supported us on Patreon: Aaron Petrie, Aaron Trueman, Adam Toplass, Adam Wright, Adam Young, Alden Siminoff, Aled Rees, Alex Crockett, Alex Day, Alex Swan, Alexandra Hamilton, Alexis Fraser, Alister Dannock, Alister Arnoch, Anand Shaunak, Andrew Citarella, Andrew JM, Andrew Johnston, Andrew MacGregor, Andrew Swan, Andy Gengler, Anne Fry, Anthony Duz, Antonio Ventre, A. Stefanick, Ashley Denneman, Belol Nessar, Ben Annowsky, Ben Balanzategui, Ben Clark, Ben Joseph, Ben Weatherburn, Benjamin Lawless, Benny Kane, Beth Higgins, Bill Milgram, Bobbi Bain, Bobby Rein, Braeden Dion, Brendan Allen, Brendan Campbell, Brian Purnell, Bruce Scrafton, Bryce Strobach, Callan Gillard, Callan Sunderland, Camille Andrea, Card Shark Comics, Carl McWinter, Carlos Perez, Carlita Dubrau, Chardee MacDennis, Charise Joy Javonillo, Charlotte Tiessen, Chris Dunnell, Chris Livingston, Chris Manning, Chris Potts, Chris Turkington, Christopher Thornthwaite, Ciaran Mitchell, Clare Dyer,

Conor Walsh, Conrad McMenamin, Corey Ferreira, Dale Cox, Dan Chalkley, Dan Shore, Dan Tom, Daniel De Voss, Daniel Johnsin, Daniel Maze, Danyon Mcneilly, Darren Dando, David Mott, David Nayer, Denholm Samaras, Dermot Sheridan, Dillon Haggett, Don Pudlowski, Doug Bogatz, Eden Babic, Eleanor Binney, Emily Gray, Fraser McLachlan, Gary Dunne, Gearoid Duane, Gearoid Harrahill, George Mills-Burrows, George Wilding, Glenn Gomes, Glenn Morton, Graham Reid, Gray Carroll, Greg Delaney, Greg Spinks, Gummy Davidson, Hamish Wilson, Hannah Reed, Hansel Tjia, Harrison Stroak, Henry Saba, Ian Astley, Isaac Morrison, Jacob Jewson, Jack Howard, Jack Missen, Jack Oliver, Jack Sharp, Jack Smith, Jack Valente, Jackson Grant, Jake Buswell, Jake Taylor, Jannon Murray, Jarrod Kerr, Jason Canham, Jason De Vincentis, Jazz Atmaja, Jennifer McKenzie, Jenny Subyak, Jeremy Fogelman, Jerry Johnson, Jessica Jobson, Jessica Olson, Jesska Davidson, Jimmy Croall, Jimmy Kennan, Jimmy Famigio, Joey Wilson, John Charin, John Harrison, John Healy, John Hoyte, John Kemp, John Klee, Jonathan Dafter, Jordan O'Meara, Jordan Wood, Joseph O'Hara, Joseph Seaton, Josh Brodrick, Justin Andrade, Justin Fintoski, Justin Fitzalan, Justin Jones, Justin White, Juztyn Crane, Kane Burt, Katherine Durant, Kathryn Ashworth, Katie Langford, Katie Marx, Kell McDonald, Kevin Coleman, Kirsty Roberts, Kris Toigo, Kyle Beech, Kynan Mugford, Lachie Dahlenburg, Lachlan Paton, Lachlan Pinder, Langdon Alger, Leon Hussain, Lewis Baisley, Lewis Bell, Liam Partlow, Liam Reid, Liam Rowe, Lorraine Cohn, Louis McAuliffe, Lucas Solon, Lucy Amos, Lucy Moore, Luis Ongpin, Luke Costin, Luke Mckay, Luke Russell,

Madeline Corzine, Marc Newby, Mark Nelson, Mark Salmon, Mark Treleaven, Martin Frederick, Marty J, Martyn Mercer, Matt Ho, Matt Taylor, Michael Chang, Michael Tricarico, Mike Altier, Mitch Dresser, Mitch Richards, Mitchell Cross, Morris Barnes, Natasha Cooper, Neil Kennedy, Niamh Gribbin, Nick Cowling, Nick Gonzalez, Nick Stuart, Nicola Carey, Nicole Kolen, Nicole Whyte, Olivia Surmon, Paddy Townsley, Pat Wright, Patrick Kennedy, Paul Downs, Paul Kelly, Paul Taylor, Paul Watts, Penelope Cohn, Pete Connell, Peter Parker, Prime Possum, Reese Patterson, Regan Ronellenfitsch, Renee Hewett, Rhydian Hughes, Rian McDonald, Richard Franks, Rob Cundari, Rob Krasa, Robb Meehan, Ronan Diamond, Ross Thompson, Ryan Winning, Sally Hayward, Sam Croese, Sam Fairbanks, Sarah Conroy, Sean O Coilain, Sean Merrigan, Seth Wiens, Shannon Hofer, Simon Brown, Simon Fathers, Sophie Smith, Stephen Falvo, Steve Hume, Steve Matthews, Steven Kind, Steven Lofthouse, Susan Plein, Tank Hafertepen, Tayler Heaney, The Rod, Thomas Mitwollen, Thomas Richardson, Thrillho, Tim Johns, Tim Jones, Tim Kadwell, Tim Slomka, Timothy Burleson, Timothy Rudiger, Tjett Gerdom, Tom Hore, Tristan Campbell, Tyler Weber, Vicky Gonzalez, Will Corneliusen, Will Holmes, William Allen.

Finally, we'd also like to thank our fellow Simpsons-based fan groups: Steven at 'Simpsons Quotes That Nobody Gets Anymore'; Cameron at 'The Simpsons Tattoo' Instagram; Carter at 'Rock Bottom'; NoHomers.Net; CompuGlobalHyperMegaNet; Simpsons Shitposting; 'The Simpsons Clips' Instagram; The Simpsons Archive; Eats Like a Duck; and Dead Homer Society.

Trivia Answers

1. 61lbs
2. Hans Moleman
3. Ice Cream
4. 25 years
5. Sir Oinks-a-lot
6. 12
7. 29
8. Martin's playhouse
9. FREDDY
10. Jacques, Mindy Simmons, Lurleen Lumpin and Princess Kashmir
11. He starts hiccuping
12. El Bombastico
13. Itchy and Scratchy Meet Fritz the Cat
14. $800 billion
15. 78
16. Lactose intolerant
17. A gold club
18. 4
19. His fife
20. The AT-5000
21. Giant rice crispy square
22. 1974
23. 9
24. Patterson, New Jersey
25. 17
26. Kid Gorgeous
27. Family, religion and friendship
28. $5
29. Purple
30. 102.5
31. Fidel Castro
32. $350
33. 59th Street Bridge
34. 1956
35. Roscoe
36. 50 cents
37. Her Nobel Peace Prize
38. Original Ray's Famous Pizza
39. Gerald Samson
40. Cesspool on the Potomac
41. Gordon 'Gordie' Howe
42. Sit On It
43. An empty can of tomato paste
44. The Duff Blimp
45. Dean Bitterman
46. A doghouse and beer
47. 17, 3, 26, 41, 38, 49
48. $59.99
49. $12.95

50. Ring toss

51. 6 a.m.

52. 25

53. Waynesport

54. Peach

55. Pyro

56. Whisky sour

57. Harrisburg Coat Outlet to buy an irregular coat

58. Will There Ever Be A Rainbow

59. Shark

60. Sonic Youth

61. Little Barbershop of Horrors

62. 40

63. Rudiger

64. Champions of winning. Superb!

65. 19

66. 18

67. Principals Do It 9 Months A Year

68. Blisstonia

69. Henry Kissinger

70. Non-alcoholic beer

71. 10

72. Apple and orange

73. 3

74. ZZ Top

75. Bigger Than Jesus

76. 1969

77. 4723 Maple Valley Road

78. Steppin' Out Fashion Mart

79. Lamp shades

80. 50 cents

81. Melvin Van Horne

82. Raspberry swirl with a double glaze

83. 96 hours

84. 12

85. 40 seconds

86. The Front

87. 6

88. 'I wish they taught shopping in school'

89. $2

90. 23

91. Cats

92. There's No Disgrace Like Home

93. Monster Mash

94. Stan 'The Boy' Taylor

95. 10 Megatons

96. Merciless peppers of Quetzlzacatenango

97. American Gothic

98. *Dr Who* marathon

99. Alfalfa

100. Tahiti

101. 42

102. 'Seeya Real Soon Kids!'

103. Roadkill 2000

104. KL5-3226

105. Walt Whitman

106. Principal Skinner
107. A noble spirit embiggens the smallest man
108. Posies
109. 107
110. Blue
111. Ray Patterson
112. Race Banyon
113. Pilot mispronouncing 'possibly'
114. The Channel 6 Wastelanders
115. 16,000 boxes of unsold wigs
116. $600

117. Mr. T
118. Compu-Global-Hyper-Mega-Net
119. $100 million
120. Geech
121. Bart
122. Skowie
123. $5000
124. Reads to the homeless
125. Green
126. Aristotle Amadopolis
127. 32
128. 1928
129. 2

130. $400
131. Benjamin, Doug and Gary
132. A Danish
133. alt.nerd. obsessive
134. Mt Useful
135. Santos L. Halper
136. Krusty's Non-Narkotic Cough Syrup
137. Two Bad Neighbours
138. Orange
139. Springfield Civic Auditorium
140. Gregory